Justice in Plainclothes

Justice in Plainclothes

A Theory of American
Constitutional Practice

Lawrence G. Sager

Yale University Press   *New Haven & London*

Production of this book was supported by the Mary Cady Tew Memorial Fund.

Library of Congress Cataloging-in-Publication Data

Sager, Lawrence G.

    Justice in plainclothes : a theory of American constitutional practice / Lawrence G. Sager.

      p.   cm.

Includes bibliographical references and index.

ISBN 0-300-10130-9 (cloth : alk. paper)

1. Constitutional law—United States. 2. Constitutional law—United States—Interpretation and construction. 3. Political questions and judicial power—United States. 4. Judicial process—United States. 5. United States—Politics and government. I. Title.

KF4550.S24 2004

342.73—dc22

2004041885

A catalogue record for this book is available from the British Library.

The paper in this book meets the guidelines for permanence and durability of the Committee on Production Guidelines for Book Longevity of the Council on Library Resources.

For Jane

Contents

Acknowledgments

The ideas in this book have been with me for a long time. In the course of this long gestation, I have accumulated many colleagues, many teachers, and many debts. I can only gesture towards those in whose debt I find myself.

I spent many years at New York University and benefited greatly from my colleagues. Ronald Dworkin and Thomas Nagel modeled intelligent discourse and normative reflection for me, and were wonderful teachers. David Richards was an unflagging source of encouragement. Francis Kamm kept us all on intellectual course. John Ferejohn and Victor Ferreres Comella brought new worlds to my understanding of the questions I take up in these pages. Lewis Kornhauser has always been the perfect friend and colleague, brimming with integrity, intelligence, and generosity. As Dean, John Sexton was always supportive of this and all my projects.

Christopher Eisgruber and I frequently complete and improve each other's thoughts and sentences, and I consider it a piece of good fortune to have him as a friend and co-author. He is remarkably able and an extraordinary pleasure to work with. There is important common ground among the constitutional thoughts of Dworkin,

Eisgruber, and me, and I have tried to note at least some of the more specific guidance I have taken from their work.

My borrowed colleagues at Boston University, where I have been a frequent visitor, were willing to play audience to my presentation of drafts on a number of occasions. Their astute and provocative responses improved my understanding of the ground over which we went together.

Dean William Powers and my new colleagues and friends at the University of Texas have made me feel wonderfully welcome and have inspired me to complete this book at last. I consider myself very lucky to have found so admirable a new academic home, and I hope that the book is worthy of it.

The ideas here have figured in formal presentations at Fordham University, Harvard University, the University of California at Berkeley, the University of Michigan, New York University, Northwestern University, the University of Pennsylvania, Pomona College, Princeton University, the University of Texas, and Yale University. And my thoughts have been greatly enriched by the many able scholars who graced the Colloquium in Constitutional Theory that Chris Eisgruber and I presided over at NYU. For inspiration, provocation, and insight in these and other contexts, including their published work, I want to single out the following figures from among the many from whom I have benefited: Bruce Ackerman, Akhil Amar, Sotirios Barber, Mitchell Berman, Robert Bone, Rebecca Brown, Richard Fallon, Jim Fleming, William Forbath, Lawrence Lessig, Sandy Levinson, Michael McConnell, Frank Michelman, Robert Post, Richard Revesz, Frederick Schauer, Riva Siegal, Cass Sunstein, Mark Tushnet, Jeremy Waldron, and Ernest Young. My thanks to all.

In his capacity as my research assistant, Josh Geller was very helpful. In like capacity, Ian Farrell and Forrest Reynolds more or less bodily carried both the manuscript and me over the finish line, for which efforts I am deeply grateful. Gavin Lewis has been a patient, subtle, and erudite editor. Ms. Susan Robbins went to great lengths to successfully rescue the manuscript from the word processor blues.

Bits and pieces—and occasionally, chunks—of this book come from previously published material. "Justice in Plainclothes" was cribbed from an article in the *Northwestern Law Review* with the same principal title, and portions of that article appear in adapted form in the text as well.[1] I have also drawn on essays that appeared in the *Fordham Law Review*,[2] the *Harvard Law Review*,[3] the *New York University Law Review*,[4] and the *New York University Journal of Legislation and Public Policy*.[5] Chapters 8 and 9, as well as a small portion of Chapter 10, derive from two essays that first appeared in collections of essays published by the Cambridge University Press.[6] I am grateful to all of these publishing entities for their earlier editorial assistance and, where required, for permission to give my work this second life.

My wife Jane Cohen, to whom this book is dedicated, made the effort possible. Among the many gifts she has given me have been the confidence and courage to see this project through. Her will, energy, intelligence, and creativity are a marvel and I borrowed from them all.

And finally, my parents. Their deep and constant fidelity to principles of justice has been an inspiration to me. I am sorry that my mother did not live to see her hopes for this book made material, and delighted that my father has.

Introduction: The Puzzle of Our Constitutional Practice

This is a book foremost about the Constitution of the United States . . . more exactly, about constitutional *practice* in the United States. A constitution without more is a piece of paper or a mythic understanding that politicians invoke in times of particularly heated rhetoric. What makes a constitution interesting is what a people do with it. In the United States, we take the Constitution seriously, and a set of traditions and institutions has developed which makes it a meaningful part of our political life. These include the written Constitution itself; our relatively robust tradition of judicial decision-making that names the Constitution as its warrant; a legacy of popular constitutional decision-making in which amendment is infrequent and constitutional language typically is both general and abstract; and the broad acceptance in our political culture of constitutional discourse as a legitimate and often preferred means of framing and resolving fundamental questions of political justice. These are all features of our constitutional practice.

At the heart of this practice there is a puzzle. Various accounts of our practice disagree on the important question of whether the Constitution contains an essentially complete set of instructions for constitutional judges or whether conscientious judges and courts must make important judgments on their own; indeed that question will be a central theme of our inquiry in these pages. But any plausible account must agree on this much: In our practice, many important constitutional choices are distributed in some fashion between two decision-making groups. On the one hand, there is the popular decision-making group—consisting of politically active persons in those few political generations that have participated in the adoption of the original Constitution or any of its amendments. On the other hand, there is the judicial decision-making group, consisting of the successive generations of judges who have had their say on questions of constitutional importance, and in particular, of the justices of the United States Supreme Court. Each of these groups is in an important way compromised. The popular group, to put the matter bluntly, is old news. Most of the important provisions of the Constitution are one or two centuries old, and the generations that participated in their drafting and ratification have long since left the stage. Without more, it is puzzling why their constitution-making acts should have so firm a grip on our contemporary political life. The judicial group raises similar concerns: Why should judges, who by design are far less accountable to popular political sentiment than are most political actors, have the capacity to unseat the decisions of elected officials or of the public at large?

To be sure, no community can start from scratch every morning. Governmental institutions have to be reasonably stable in order that a people can go about their lives with some degree of assurance that their government can govern. With or without a written constitution, a political community has to settle on its governing institutions, and is advantaged if it can live by the major terms of its settlement for a reasonably long period of time. All successful political communities have important inertial characteristics; indeed, we might say that in this sense all successful political communities have constitutions.

But what dominates and distinguishes constitutional activity in the United States is not just or even primarily concern with the basic institutions of government. At the heart of our practice are what we can call the *liberty-bearing* provisions of the Constitution—provisions concerned not so much with the structure of government as with the substance of governmental behavior and its relationship to the legitimate demands of members of our political community that they be treated justly. The liberty-bearing provisions include: the Bill of Rights in general and the guarantees of free expression and religious liberty in the First Amendment in particular; the antislavery provisions of the Thirteenth Amendment; the guarantees of fair process, independence, and equal citizenship of the Fourteenth Amendment; the insistence on the fair distribution of the right to vote in the Fifteenth, Nineteenth, and Twenty-Sixth Amendments; and, from the body of the original Constitution, the prohibition of bills of attainder and ex post facto laws.

However persuasive we find the claim for the inevitable inertia of the structural features of government, that claim has little force when applied to the important and often controversial questions which preoccupy the liberty-bearing provisions of the Constitution. Political cultures often will have strong traditions associated with matters of political justice, but in their very nature these matters call for dynamic rather than static responses. And here, at least, the puzzle of our constitutional practice has real bite: Why are we prepared to concede decisions about fundamental questions of political justice to a combination of ancient constitution-making majorities and contemporary courts?

This puzzle of our constitutional practice has worried several generations of constitutional judges and scholars, but has never been laid comfortably to rest. We ought to treat the challenge of this puzzle seriously. The Constitution, after all, has a unique status in our political life, and our constitutional practice is increasingly the object of admiration and emulation. But at the same time that our constitutional practice has become one of our most important institutional exports, its status at home is distinctly troubled. It has become commonplace for political leaders and groups of persons committed to various causes to react to specific Supreme Court decisions or broad lines of precedent in extreme and hyperbolic ways. There are regular calls for amendments that would fine-tune judicial readings of our constitutional tradition, calls which if taken seriously would drastically demote the role of the judiciary in giving stable shape to the realization of constitutional values. The flag-burning and school prayer amendment efforts are good examples.[1] In the midst of these amendment controversies, very few voices were raised on behalf of our constitutional practice as the general means of getting good answers to fundamental questions of political justice. Very few political leaders, whatever their position on the underlying merits, raised what should have been a salient—albeit nondecisive—objection to these amendments, namely, that tinkering at the margins of judicially accepted constitutional outcomes was a doubtful, perhaps even dangerous practice upon which to embark.

Politicians and academics who can agree on little else have made common cause in calling for radical revisions of our constitutional practice. More or less serious proposals have been floated to give Congress a legislative veto over Supreme Court decisions or even to abolish judicial review. On a different but related front, some scholars are firmly of the view that the seemingly well-settled stipulations within Article V for the amendment of the Constitution are misshaped and inappropriately stringent—and possibly even vulnerable to periodic circumvention by a determined electorate.[2] Common to these signs of fairly deep discomfort with things as they are is the worry that extant constitutional practice is undemocratic.

None of this is new, of course: The Supreme Court has not infrequently been the target of political attack or slightly more be-

nign scholarly probes, and the charge that the Court is an undemocratic institution has not infrequently been the weapon or instru-
ment of choice.[3] But for all of this sound and occasional fury, the
Court has survived, and its role in our political life seems secure.
Even some of the Court's most energetic contemporary critics acknowledge that their complaints are unlikely to have any operational
significance.[4]

Still, we owe it to ourselves, and to those who look to our example for guidance, to better understand the conceptual foundations of
what we do. More than intellectual completeness is at stake. The
broad contours of our practice may be quite secure, but at the
margins there is considerable disarray. The justices of the Supreme
Court are in radical disagreement about their role in finding or
creating constitutional meaning; doctrine about the relationship between the Court and other constitutional actors appears to be in the
midst of a seismic shift;[5] and, in general, the sense that we as a
political community are embarked on a common constitutional
project—a project that helps give shape and value to our political
life—seems for the moment to be ebbing. We would do well to better
explain ourselves to ourselves.

The Justice-Seeking Account

This book aims at such an explanation. At its heart is the idea of
partnership or collaboration. Judges, for their part, are not merely
or even primarily instruction-takers; their independent normative
judgment is expected and welcomed. They are in a relationship of
partnership with those persons in the founding or amending generations who participated in the framing of the Constitution's text, not
merely their agents. This partnership has a characteristic structure:
At least with regard to the liberty-bearing provisions of the Constitution, the popular constitutional decision-maker typically speaks at a

high level of generality and of moral abstraction. The job of the constitutional judiciary thus becomes applying very general constitutional commitments to concrete cases, with the concomitant obligations of generating case-spanning doctrine and moral understandings which choose among competing accounts of the Constitution's lofty norms. The object of this partnership is the project of bringing our political community into better conformity with fundamental requirements of political justice. This is the nub of the justice-seeking account of our constitutional practice.

But if that is how we are to regard our constitutional practice, what are we to make of the prominent and enduring moral deficiencies of constitutional doctrine? Consider, for example, these two propositions: that members of our political community are entitled to economic arrangements that offer them minimally decent material lives in exchange for hard work; and that government is obliged to make reasonable efforts to undo structurally entrenched social bias against vulnerable racial groups and women. Neither of these principles—the right to minimum welfare or the obligation to reform entrenched bias—has now or has ever had any apparent life in constitutional doctrine. They seem, however, all but unduckable requirements of political justice.

The justice-seeking account offers two structural explanations for the durable moral shortfall of constitutional doctrine. The first is this: There is and should be a gap between the Constitution itself and the judicially enforced Constitution. The Constitution is underenforced by the judiciary, and for good reason. The right to minimum welfare and the obligation to reform structurally entrenched social bias are in fact two good examples of such underenforcement. They are good examples because they depend for their implementation upon a complex set of choices of strategy and responsibility, and these supervening choices ought to be made, as a matter of both principle and sensible practice, by popular political institutions. Wrapped as they are in questions beyond the competence of the judiciary, these claims for constitutional justice are, in the first instance, the obligation of popular political institutions, not the courts.

A second important constitutional collaboration is thus invoked by the justice-seeking account of our constitutional practice. Constitutional judges are part of a contemporary partnership with popular governmental actors which promises more complete constitutional justice than could be realized by the courts alone. The Court on this account has several responsibilities, however. Above all, it should welcome rather than eschew the collaborative efforts of other actors, especially the Congress of the United States; where those other actors have put in place positive programs that have constitutional justice as their end, the Court should police those programs for the arbitrary exclusion of individuals or for unjust categorical exclusions; and the Court should guard against deformations of traditional governmental structures that work to the disadvantage of vulnerable groups who depend on nonjudicial governmental actors for full protection against injustice. Underenforcement is not just about selective judicial passivity, accordingly; it charts a course of secondary action by the Court, action in service of the efforts of the nonjudicial actors to realize constitutional justice.

Judicial underenforcement of the Constitution is only part of the explanation for the moral shortfall of constitutional law. The domain of constitutional justice—even to the extent that it eludes judicial enforcement—is more limited than the domain of full political justice, and certainly more limited than the domain of best outcomes generally. Some important questions—for example, the relative value of park land, art museums, and athletic facilities—depend in principle on the aggregate wishes of the members of our political community. Other important questions may not in principle depend upon popular will but may still be properly assigned to the popular political process in a well-functioning democracy. Many questions that may fall under the rubric of political justice are fact-specific, time-dependent, and/or legitimately subject to competing priorities. It is neither appropriate nor sound as a matter of social strategy to extend constitutional justice to matters such as these. To function effectively as the political conscience of a democratic people, a constitution's liberty-bearing precepts must be spare, durable, and relatively nonnegotiable. Hence the need for triage, for focusing on the most urgent and enduring concerns of political union.

Not surprisingly, therefore, few constitutional observers believe that the Constitution requires perfect economic justice, whatever their view of what that state of affairs would be. But the need for spare, durable, and categorical constitutional precepts does not exclude all questions of material well-being from the domain of constitutional justice. Surely no prosperous community that fails to offer its members who are willing to work the opportunity to secure materially decent lives for themselves and their families can be regarded as just. And without the guarantee of such an opportunity to thrive, the promise of more abstract political rights seems painfully empty. So some version of this minimal demand for the opportunity of material gain is within the domain of constitutional justice, albeit in a form that is generally elusive of judicial enforcement.

There is one other feature of the justice-seeking account of our constitutional practice: Article V of the Constitution requires the support of a supermajority of the states for any amendment, much as Article VII required such a supermajority for the launching of the Constitution initially. It was anticipated that the Constitution would be hard to amend, and in practice it has been remarkably so. Far from regarding this obduracy to change as an embarrassment, the justice-seeking account sees it as a virtue: By forcing would-be popular constitutional decision-makers to secure broad interstate and interregional consensus, and by making them aware that they are drafting not just for themselves but for their children and their children's children, Article V inspires constitutional choices of the right kind. It inspires, that is, the choice of widely acceptable, general, and abstract precepts, precepts which in turn facilitate the working partnership with the constitutional judiciary that we have considered in the preceding paragraphs.

The justice-seeking view of our constitutional institutions depends upon the belief that ongoing, precedent-respecting judicial judgment—guided only broadly by the text of the Constitution—is a reasonably good guide to the most critical requirements of political justice. This is an impossibly complex judgment of institutional competence, and in the end we may have only impressions of our national experience and the experience of other modern states and guesses as to how those experiences might otherwise have gone upon which to rely. But there are distinct features of constitutional adjudication that should give us some reason for confidence in that process as the pragmatic means of helping us to recognize and respect the precepts of justice; the identification and defense of those features is an important task of the justice-seeking account.

This, then, is the general picture of the justice-seeking Constitution: Constitutional judges are partners rather than agents, and are expected to do much of the heavy normative lifting in the course of bringing detail to the abstract generalities of the liberty-bearing portions of the Constitution. Some important requirements of the Constitution are judicially underenforced; but recognition of that circumstance sponsors a distinct judicial role in making it possible for nonjudicial actors to join the enterprise of constitutional justice. The domain of constitutional justice is far from exhaustive of all of political justice, but includes at least a minimal insistence on the opportunity to secure a materially decent life. And, in combination, these arrangements and understandings are reasonably well suited to the project of bringing us as a people closer to compliance with the most urgent concerns of political justice. In this book, I attempt to elaborate and defend this picture.

Three Disclaimers

This undertaking must necessarily be a modest one. I do not mean to suggest that the concerns and disagreements which presently roil the waters of our constitutional practice are simply matters of lingering confusion, and that a little clear thinking will put matters to rest. These questions are dense and complex, and well laced with political controversy. But anyone entering this conversation ought to do so in the spirit of reason rather than rhetoric, and with assumptions favoring the good faith and seriousness of the other participants, however sharp the disagreements among them may be. It is in that spirit that I set out here.

The reader will have already discovered that I am, on the whole, sympathetic to the broad structural features of our constitutional practice. Compared to many contemporary commentators, I am optimistic about the Constitution and generous in my view of the capacity and authority of constitutional judges. But I emphatically do not mean to argue that our practice is perfect for us or ideal for any other of the world's peoples. I mean only to claim that our practice represents a reasonably good choice for a people such as ourselves—a plural people for whom justice matters. This judgment is ultimately a pragmatic one and a rough one at that. Our Constitution, like any to which we could possibly be attracted, aims at matters of deep principle; but our Constitution, like any that could be, must realize that aim through entirely fallible mechanisms.

I certainly do not want to be understood as suggesting that we inhabit the best of all worlds, that we are as well composed as we should be, or even that the Constitution has made the best contribution to us that it could have done or could in the future do. On the contrary, I think that we could do much better with what we have—with the Constitution as it is written, with our constitutional tradition as it can best be understood, and with the constitutional judiciary as it is presently composed and often regarded. The purpose of this book is to bring us closer to the best version of ourselves as we find ourselves, not to apologize or gloss over our constitutional shortcomings.

Finally, even in the best of all constitutional worlds, a constitution can only do so much, can only set the table for a democratic people. To the partisans in contemporary debates over euthanasia, gay rights, the rights of criminal defendants, affirmative action, single-sex education, and educational vouchers, it might sometimes seem that the asserted authority of the constitutional judiciary is pervasive and omnipotent. But the reach of the constitutional judiciary is finite indeed, and almost no one holds otherwise. Almost no one believes, for example, that the Supreme Court should control military policy, regulate banks, or preside over fiscal or developmental policy generally.

In the end, whether we succeed at any of our goals as a people—and most particularly, whether we succeed in our quest for a just society—will depend on us and our progeny in political interaction. This book is simply about the sort of help we can hope to get from our Constitution in the course of our efforts.

CHAPTER 1

Accounts of Our Constitutional Practice

What We Can Expect of an
Account of Our Constitutional Practice

The project of this book is the development of the "justice-
seeking account" of our constitutional practice. I've chosen
the somewhat informal idea of an *account* in part to avoid
being drawn into too lengthy a discussion of methodology. I hope
not to succumb to the temptation to engage in the kind of conceptual throat-clearing that defers substance far too long. Still, we
need some idea of what an account of our constitutional practice or
any other social practice is meant to be, and what it is meant to
accomplish.

An account of a social practice is an articulate understanding of
the dominant features of that practice. A successful account is one
that explains why if at all we should regard the practice as valuable
and how we should maintain or reshape the practice at its margins
in order to make it as valuable as possible to us—members of the
society in which the practice is lodged.

All this seems innocent enough, but even so modest and straightforward an ambition as an account on this reading sets loose some

important and possibly confounding complications. If we set out to understand an ongoing practice with the object of knowing better what is valuable about that practice we necessarily find ourselves straddling the divide between what *is* and what *ought to be.* Or perhaps the better metaphor is longitudinal: We find ourselves with our feet on the ground of things as they are and with our heads in the clouds of things as they ought to be.

This creates an ongoing tension between the extant particular and the valued universal of a sort that is characteristic of much discourse within legal studies and—more generally, within normative political science or political theory. In these areas, typically a very concrete and necessarily messy, flawed object is on the table— say, the law of contracts or the U.S. Congress. But persuasive arguments about how best to understand the object in question, and how best to maintain or reform the constituent parts of that object will depend upon much more general and idealized notions of what is valuable. In such an exercise it is inevitable and important that the general inquiry into justification and the particular inquiry into fit have substantial influence over each other. One's justifications, while appealing to general propositions of political justice or practice, will to some degree be inspired and shaped to the particular practice; and one's view of the actual practice will be through the lens of the most apparently persuasive justifications for that practice. If an account of a social practice is successful it will be precisely because the ends and means have more or less been made to meet.

This may at times encourage readers and even authors to overread accounts of legal doctrine, political institutions, or complex practices like constitutionalism. Typically, even an attractive and persuasive account will justify no proposition more robust than that a well-formed and well-intentioned political community like the one in which the practice in question is presently alive would have a good reason to adopt or continue the practice, along with a prescription for guiding the development of that practice in the future. But the introduction of general arguments about what is valuable will tempt both readers and authors to conceive of the practice as essential to human flourishing or better than any rival practice, or at least better than any rival practice in the community under study. This is more than most accounts can claim, and almost certainly more than any account of constitutional practice in the United States can claim. After all, we have the chronic example of the English regime of parliamentary supremacy to humble our ambitions.

True, I hope in these pages to offer an account of our constitutional practice that will shed light not just on the questions of what good reasons we have for pursuing that practice and the best means of doing so; I hope as well to offer reasons why other political communities should be attracted to practices roughly like ours, and insight into the structure of constitutional practice more generally. But no account of constitutional practice can offer itself as universal or ideal, and I do not have that unattainable ambition here. Nor, as I emphasized at the outset, do I believe or mean to argue that we inhabit the best of all constitutional worlds. The justice-seeking account of our practice should above all explain our practice to ourselves in a way that will help us recognize its value and move in the direction of correcting its faults.

Agency and Partnership Accounts of Constitutional Practice

We can better understand the substance and force of the justice-seeking account by locating that account among its actual and possible competitors. A useful way of cataloging such accounts is by focusing upon their characterization of the role of constitutional judges. Judges are not the only constitutional actors, of course; indeed, some of the most important propositions of which I hope to persuade you depend upon a renunciation of our too common association of what judges do with the whole of our constitutional practice. But judges are very important constitutional actors, and some of the most important differences between competing accounts of our practice are the implications of those accounts for the behavior of responsible judges.

We can start with the division between *agency* and *partnership* accounts of the role of constitutional judges. In agency accounts, the idealized judge is an agent of other decision-makers; she is an instruction-taker. The source or sources of the instruction varies among these accounts, but is likely to include some combination of constitutional text, context, the intent of the framers (or more plausibly the framing generations) of the pertinent constitutional text, and deeply embedded tradition. More important, perhaps, is what must be excluded from the ideal instruction set of judges in order to maintain their role as agents: Just as agents in general are not expected to pursue their own interests, judges on the agency account are expected to renounce the authority of their independent normative judgment, unless that judgment is somehow invoked by the role of instruction-taking itself. (This last proviso may seem obscure and undermining; we will come to an explanation shortly, when we consider reluctant judgment theories—a group of agency accounts that admit judicial judgment into the picture, but only grudgingly.)

Partnership accounts, in contrast, treat judges as partners or collaborators in the enterprise of establishing and giving operational content to precepts of constitutional value. Partnership models value judges precisely because of the normative judgment they bring to the table. That judgment is bounded and disciplined by the constitutional sources invoked in agency accounts, and by the complex and somewhat inertial protocols of adjudication as well. But, in the end, judicial judgment is welcomed as an important virtue of our constitutional arrangements rather than as an embarrassment.

There is, or at least conceptually could be, a third broad class of accounts of our constitutional practice, which we could call the *guardianship* model. The idea of judicial guardianship would be that we as a political community have placed ourselves in a kind of moral receivership, and given to judges the largely unbridled authority to guide our affairs, at least insofar as those affairs implicate questions of political justice, broadly conceived. I speak here in the subjunctive, because I am aware of no serious accounts of our constitutional practice that gesture towards this sort of primary, undisciplined, and unshared authority. But I mention the paradigm of guardianship for two reasons. First, it brings conceptual completeness to our catalog of possible accounts. Second, many of those who reject partnership accounts may ignore the difference between judicial partnership and guardianship, or may believe that the justice-seeking view and others like it are guardianship wolves in partnership clothing.

But we are in danger of getting ahead of ourselves. Agency, partnership, and guardianship designate broad readings of our constitutional practice, not specific accounts or even recognizable families or forms of accounts. We need to get more specific.

Pure Agency: Originalism

Among agency accounts we can distinguish between a pure form and a moderated form. The pure form of the agency account is *originalism*. Originalist accounts see the content of the Constitution as laid down at identifiable moments in the past by popular political events of particular sorts, and see the job of giving meaning to the Constitution as one of recovering or excavating material deposited in these past constitutional moments. Originalist accounts are open to contemporary reflection on the advantages and limitations of our constitutional institutions, but the normative content of these reflections does not bleed into the interpretation of the Constitution itself. The only link between contemporary normative judgment and the protocol of constitutional interpretation recognized by originalist accounts is in this sense self-denying. An originalist might well argue, for example, that it is undemocratic for judges to permit their own values or judgments to determine the outcome of constitutional controversies, and that judicial inquiry must for precisely that reason confine itself to the enterprise of deciphering past constitution-making events.

In the originalist account, constitutional architecture is elementary. We can imagine the universe of possible collective political decisions: All of these decisions are in a sense made under the aegis of the Constitution, but most are commended by the Constitution to various more or less popular political entities. Some of these entities (like Congress) are created by the Constitution itself; others (like the states and their political institutions) are inherited or incorporated by the Constitution. Many of these entities are open to change by other state or federal political processes in ways that are largely unrestricted by the federal Constitution. In all, most of the matters that attract our collective attention are left open by the Constitution; the remainder comprises nothing more nor less than the comparatively small subset of political matters concluded by the historic Constitution. For the originalist, constitutional interpretation is the backward-looking enterprise of decoding the text and circumstances of the Constitution's authorship to reveal the meaning lodged there. The Constitution on this view picks up and leaves off just as and because the framers took up and left off, whatever the cause: arbitrary choice, oversight, political pressure, or simply fatigue.

Moderated Agency:
Reluctant Judgment Theories

Originalism's stern conceptual boundaries on the role of the constitutional judiciary are dramatically relaxed in several recent analyses that we might call *reluctant judgment* accounts of our constitutional practice. Reluctant judgment theorists, at least on the surface, are originalist in aspiration; that is, if the historical Constitution offered a stable and applicable mandate that judges could access without bringing to bear their independent moral judgment, these theorists would regard that circumstance as preferable. Unfortunately, these theorists observe, things are not like that. To be faithful to the mandate of the Constitution judges need to bring some independent moral judgment to bear.

This might be so because the mandate uttered in one era has to be translated in a modern milieu where many things have changed, including the conceptual paradigms by which we understand our world. Or it might be so because—appropriately understood—the Constitution contains broad, overlapping, and partially conflicting mandates, which must be reconciled or synthesized by judges committed to taking their instructions from the Constitution. What these models or metaphors of translation and synthesis have in common is a basal, unmitigated commitment to agency in principle, coupled with the realization that pure agency in constitutional adjudication is impossible. The instructions of the historical Constitution have to be translated or reconciled, and that secondary enterprise inevitably engages the independent normative judgment of constitutional judges. It would be self-defeating to exclude these judgmental ingredients of adjudication, because the result would be a decision that was less rather than more faithful to the instructions of the past. Paradoxically, precisely because she has set out to be a good instruction-taker—an agent for our constitutional past—the conscientious constitutional judge must make many important decisions on her own. "Reluctant judgment" seems an apt label for accounts of our constitutional practice which assume this general form, because judgment enters the story as an afterthought, as an inevitable but unfortunate limit on the instruction-taking impulse.

Even now, of course, we are painting with rather broad strokes. But with the further division of agency accounts into pure originalist and reluctant judgment theories, we have enough for our present purposes. We can turn now to the partnership side of this conceptual divide.

Pure Partnership: The Justice-Seeking Accounts

Just as originalism is the pure form of agency, the justice-seeking account of our constitutional practice is the pure form of partnership. I have already introduced the reader to the justice-seeking view in brief, and much of the remainder of this book is an attempt to consider our constitutional practice from that vantage. I only want here to be to clear about the distinction between the justice-seeking account and its rivals.

The justice-seeking view values the active partnership of the constitutional judiciary on the grounds that judicial judgment guided broadly by the text of the Constitution will steer us reasonably well in the enterprise of bringing our political community better into conformity with fundamental requirements of political justice. On this view, judges are not confined to the role of taking instructions in some mechanical sense; neither, it should be emphasized, are they constrained to the role of "translating" instructions from a culturally different past or of synthesizing overlapping and conflicting instructions from different constitutional epochs. These more subtle understandings of constitutional judges as instruction-takers still regard the role of the constitutional judge as that of being the best instruction-taker she can be, and make room for the independent normative judgment of constitutional judges and courts only grudgingly, as the paradoxical and unfortunate consequence of the instruction-taking venture. Justice-seeking constitutionalism, in contrast, welcomes and values the independent judgmental role of judges as reasonably well-suited to the enterprise that is its namesake.

On the other flank, justice-seeking constitutionalism is importantly distinct from judicial guardianship as well. In the partnership between constitutional judges and the popular constitutional decision-maker, the latter is the senior partner. Where constitutional text speaks clearly, judges are obliged to respond. Academics bent on unseating the idea that text can bind its interpreters have played with the idea that even the constitutionally specified age limits for high national office are subject to wide-ranging understandings; but these are the games of academics. When Julian Bond was nominated for the office of Vice President at the 1968 Democratic National Convention, but withdrew because he was younger than the minimum required age for that office, he and his supporters understood the Constitution to mean precisely what it said. So too must judges, when the Constitution is clear and firm. Even liberty-bearing provisions can be firm in this way: Ready examples include the Seventh Amendment's guarantee of the right to a jury trial,[1] and the considerably less arithmetic stipulation of birthright citizenship in the Fourteenth Amendment.[2] So too, most if not all of the proposals to amend the Constitution in order to make anti–flag-burning laws constitutional would have achieved their ends if enacted, notwithstanding a Supreme Court which thought them a serious constitutional mistake. Even extremely plastic and contestable constitutional concepts may bind judges firmly at their core: No judge after the enactment of the Thirteenth and Fourteenth Amendments could defend governmental behavior against constitutional challenge on the grounds that our political culture recognizes or tolerates the supremacy of one race over another, even if her un-bound judgment strongly favored so ugly a view.

To say that the popular constitutional decision-maker can sharply limit or even eliminate the range of reasonable disagreement about the meaning of the Constitution with regard to a range of cases, and hence can bind conscientious judges, is not to say that we are better off when judges are so bound. On the contrary, justice-seeking con-stitutionalism values the independent normative judgment of judges as a central reason for having a Constitution with liberty-bearing provisions. But constitutional text and context are important sources of the discipline of judicial judgment, a discipline which distin-guishes justice-seeking judicial practice from guardianship.

A second major discipline of decisions by the constitutional ju-diciary comes from the nature of the judicial process. By "judicial process" here, I mean to comprehend a variety of features of ad-judication: the call of appropriately positioned parties on the atten-tion of the constitutional judiciary; the common law protocol of adjudication pursuant to which the decision of a matter before a court must be justified with regard to past decisions and in turn projects a burden of justification on future decisions; the articulate giving of publicly defensible reasons for decision; the collegial na-ture of state supreme courts and of the Supreme Court of the United States; and the focused and redundant nature of judicial inquiry into governmental compliance with the Constitution. All these features of the judicial process shape the outcomes of that process, and serve to sharply distinguish that process from unbridled guardianship.

Moderated Partnership: Democratarian Theories

Like judicial agency, judicial partnership has a moderated form; we can call it *democratarian* theory. Democratarian accounts acknowledge and value the substantial play of independent judicial judgment in our constitutional practice, but they seek to limit the play of that judgment in a particular way. Democratarians hold that the play of active judicial judgment must be confined to the enterprise of improving the democratic process—or perhaps it would be better to say, to the enterprise of making our political community more fully democratic. Democratarians often claim to be the beneficiaries of a kind of conceptual judo, in which the force of the democratic objection to a robust judicial role is turned against itself: Surely, the argument goes, no one could object on democratic grounds to judicial activity that is aimed at improving democracy.

Democratarians vary considerably in their ideas of what democracy requires, from a relatively spare insistence on well-structured majoritarian institutions to far more generous views of what it is that a commitment to democracy entails.

A Spectrum of Understandings

The diagram below provides a rough map of this taxonomy of views of our constitutional practice. Because these views are distinguished not by disagreements about the ultimate substance of constitutional meaning, but rather by the connection of constitutional judges to that substance, their place on this map connects only indirectly and imperfectly to the question of how strong a presence in our political life judicial decisions that claim the warrant of constitutional authority might have. A constitutional judge who was strongly committed to the implausibly extreme model of guardianship, for example, might hold other surprising views, including the belief that persons' opportunity to speak their minds was a value that should be routinely sacrificed to other social goals, and further, that legislatures were reasonably reliable mechanisms for deciding when such a sacrifice should take place; such a judge would be very reluctant to

AGENCY		PARTNERSHIP		GUARDIANSHIP
Originalism	Reluctant Judgement l	Democratarian	Justice-Seeking l	?
More restrictive < -- > *Less restrictive*				

intervene in legislative decisions which many would see as flagrantly violating the norms of free speech. There would be more bells and whistles in a justice-seeking judge's thought process, but her results too could be very wide-ranging, though less so than those of a guardian. A democratarian judge could have a very wide or very narrow view of what democracy requires; so too a reluctant judgment jurist whose idea of what concerns were packed into the requirements of translation could vary substantially. Still, these categories clearly describe different paths of reflection, and move from more to less restrictive views of the abstract range of matters that are properly the object of a judge's reflection.

Are We All Justice-Seekers?

The reader may wonder if these categories hold against the objection that we all are at root justice-seekers. The argument would run like this: A persuasive defense of even the most value-restricted judicial role, originalism, would depend upon a view of what political justice requires of our political community and how we can best achieve that. Some view of what decisions should be conceded to democratic majorities, for example, will almost certainly be central to the case for this pure form of agency. So an originalist theorist is asking the same kind of question as the justice-seeking theorist, just getting different answers. The same point can be made from the perspective of a constitutional judge who is deciding what her role ought to be. If she is thoughtful, she cannot renounce questions of political justice at the outset; if anything will lead her to a normative judgment–blocking role like originalism, it will be her own normative judgment. (Well, possibly the precedent of her predecessors' view of their role might do this work; but if she is thoughtful, our judge will need a reason to follow that precedent, not to mention a strong value-forged lens through which to view it. And so forth.) The observation that we are all in the same normative soup is both true and important. Important, because the proponents of such restrictive accounts of the role of constitutional judges have to join in the discourse about political justice and the means of realizing it; they cannot invoke a majoritarian vision of democracy as somehow above or behind this broad normative inquiry. Nor can they be abiding skeptics about the existence and accessibility of norms of political justice, since they are almost certainly constrained to invoke such norms directly as constraints on the choice of institutional arrangements or indirectly as the goal against which the efficacy of institutional arrangements is to be measured. Imagine, for example, a constitutional theorist who insists that claims about the justness of—for example—the state barring the use of contraceptives by married couples, can be sensibly understood only as the preferences of the persons advancing such claims for living in a society of a particular sort. Accordingly, our not altogether hypothetical theorist goes on to insist, such questions can only be resolved appropriately by an elected assembly. Without more, this is an incoherent position. Our theorist believes in some strong principles of political justice, to wit, in principles that demand that an elected assembly make certain important political choices. His dismissal of the claim that justice demands that citizens be independent of the state's dictates under the circumstances of *Griswold v. Connecticut*[3] cannot, therefore, rest upon the ground that there is no truth in matters of justice or that matters of political justice have no bottom upon which political choice can rest.[4]

But it does not follow from the shared need to appeal to normative propositions that accounts of our constitutional practice are indistinct from one another. Originalist, reluctant judgment, justice-seeking and (hypothetically) guardianship accounts are plainly and crucially different in their understanding of what institutional arrangements can best serve the deep and enduring interests of our political community. They produce markedly divergent prescriptions for judicial conduct, ranging along a spectrum largely defined by the degree to which questions of political justice are open or foreclosed to the conscientious constitutional judge.

These divergent accounts are likely to reflect deeper differences in fundamental ideas about the requirements of political justice; they do not, however, flow as directly from such fundamental distinctions as at least some theorists—uncomfortable, as many of us are, with the messiness of practical judgments about concrete institutional arrangements—seem to believe. Some originalists, for example, see abstract arguments about the requirements of democracy as decisive reasons for accepting the constraints of the originalist protocol. Conversely, some justice-seeking theorists seem at least at times to believe that their view of political justice—often a rival view of the requirements of democracy—offers a decisive or nearly decisive reason for adopting their much more generous view of the role of the constitutional judiciary. A leitmotif of the analysis upon which we are about to embark in the chapters that follow is skepticism about these too-quick moves from political philosophy to constitutional accounts of institutional role.

The rough structure of my skepticism in this regard is this. Those originalists who claim the direct warrant of political theory have (and must have) an extremely crabbed and deeply implausible view of the fundamental requirements of political justice. The best justice-seeking theorists are more persuasive on the theoretical front, to be sure; but the most that their theories can do is release us from the theoretical constraints invoked by the originalists. Still open is the question of institutional design, a question laced with pragmatic concerns. Political theory can deliver us from the conceptual constraints of originalism, and motivate our concern for a robust and effective set of institutions; but there remains the need to understand why we might be reasonably optimistic about a justice-seeking constitutional judiciary. This is not meant to be an argument, merely the announcement of a theme that will thread itself through the discussion that follows.

Are We All Agency Theorists?

I may have persuaded my critical reader that these diverse accounts of our constitutional practice do not collapse into justice-seeking, only to generate the opposite concern, namely, that they all collapse into one or another form of the agency model. Judicial partnership is distinct from judicial guardianship, after all, precisely because it recognizes the discipline imposed upon judicial decisions by traditional legal sources, including the discipline of the enacted Constitution. In the partnership between the popular constitutional decision-maker (the political community that framed and ratified a portion of the Constitution) and the constitutional judiciary, the popular decision-maker is the senior partner: The space for the independent normative judgment of the constitutional judiciary is described by the normative latitude or generality of the provisions of the enacted Constitution, as fairly understood.

Accordingly, there is a sense in which all plausible accounts of the role of the constitutional judiciary treat judges as instruction-takers (I do not take possible guardianship accounts to be in the realm of the plausible). So understood, the difference between originalist, reluctant judgment, democratarian, and justice-seeking theorists is a difference in their understanding of the nature of the instructions emanating from the enacted Constitution, a disagreement that is particularly deep with regard to the liberty-bearing features of the Constitution.

Judges or theorists committed to one or another of these accounts could indeed have different understandings of the nature of the Constitution's instructions, and the difference in their readings of these instructions could be an important part of what draws them to the view that they hold. At the justice-seeking end of the spectrum in particular, there is a necessary link between the instructions ascribed to the Constitution and the contemplated judicial role: Justice-seekers have to see the liberty-bearing provisions and the Constitution as a whole as requiring or at least permitting them to exercise their normative judgment over a substantial range of matters associated with the fundamental requirements of political justice.

But it would be a mistake to think that disparate readings of the Constitution's text exhaust or are necessarily at the root of the differences among accounts of our constitutional practice. Were we to focus on the disparity of readings at play in this context, we would quickly discover that this divergence itself typically rests upon different normative views that judges and theorists bring to the job of reading the Constitution. And that would only be the beginning of the deeper, structural differences we would encounter.

Higher-order principles of construction—which may or may not derive support from the enacted Constitution per se—are an important part of what separates these distinct accounts of constitutional practice. One such higher-order principle addresses the question of how judges should respond to the enacted Constitution when text and context leave important questions of scope and application to be worked through. (What groups besides the then newly freed slaves should be beneficiaries of the Equal Protection Clause? Is affirmative action required, tolerated, or generally eschewed on the best reading of the Equal Protection Clause?) The originalist is likely committed—at least nominally—to what we could call the clear instruction rule: If the Constitution's command is clear beyond doubt, follow it; if not, leave the Constitution out of the picture, and allow the popular political process to go forward. The justice-seeker, in contrast, is likely committed to what we could call the "best judgment rule": Come to the best available understanding of, for example, constitutional equality, and develop doctrine to serve that understanding. The democratarian is likely to have a split-level approach: If the matter before the Court concerns the requirements of a well-formed democracy, act as would a justice-seeker; otherwise, act as would an originalist.

A related but distinct higher-order rule of construction concerns two different understandings of the status of the liberty-bearing provisions of the Constitution. The originalist must see them as specific instructions; the justice-seeker may see them quite differently, as instantiations of a project of seeking out the fundamental requirements of political justice, a project which the conscientious constitutional judge is obliged to pursue.

Back to the Heart of the Matter

There is a lesson to be taken from these two accordion-like exercises of pushing the different accounts of our constitutional practice together and then pulling them apart again. Of course any attractive understanding of our constitutional practice will have a normative foundation. No sensible constitutional theorist or responsible constitutional judge can think that his or her enterprise is unconnected with the pursuit of political justice. And of course any attractive understanding of our practice will require judges to attend to the instructions of the enacted Constitution. Originalism cannot be dismissed as implausibly indifferent to justice; and justice-seeking constitutional theory cannot be dismissed as celebrating the gnomic utterances of detached guardians.

But there remains a substantial conceptual and practical gulf among originalist, reluctant judgment, democratarian, and justice-seeking accounts of our constitutional practice. The choice among them, inevitably, will take us back to bedrock questions of constitutional purpose and institutional design. Why do we have a Constitution, and why do we value a constitutional practice that takes some important questions out of the hands of the popular political process and distributes authority over them to some combination of the historic political decisions that produced the enacted Constitution, on the one hand, and the decisions of contemporary constitutional judges on the other?

CHAPTER 2

Judges as Agents of the Past:
The Burdens of Originalism

Agency theories of the Constitution enjoy the great advantage of appealing to a simple and widely held model of the connection between judges and authoritative legal texts: The law speaks, and judges obey, full stop. The originalist protocol seems the unexceptional embodiment of this simple truth about the structure of legal authority. What more need be said on behalf of originalism, with its strict insistence that constitutional judges confine themselves to the instructions of the enacted Constitution?

Rather a lot, actually. This blunt claim on behalf of originalism both misses important truths about the way that ordinary legislation works, and ignores significant differences between ordinary legislation and the Constitution. We have already glimpsed the ways in which the question of textual authority is considerably more complicated than the simple command-response model sometimes invoked on behalf of originalism, when we observed that all plausible constitutional theories respect the authority of the enacted Constitution, but nevertheless diverge radically in their view of the responsibilities of the conscientious judge. We can now look more deeply at the sources of that disagreement among authority-respecting accounts of our constitutional practice.

Legislation

The Sherman Antitrust Act makes illegal "combinations in restraint of trade";[1] the Equal Employment Opportunities Act makes it unlawful for employers "to discriminate against any individual . . . because of such individual's race, color, religion, sex or national origin";[2] and the Voting Rights Act prohibits the imposition by any State or political subdivision of a "voting qualification or prerequisite to voting or standard, practice or procedure . . . which results in a denial or abridgement of the right of any citizen of the United States to vote on account of race or color."[3] Each of these provisions has quite predictably spawned a substantial jurisprudence. Even the pertinent guiding principles—as to what it is in general that makes a business arrangement a combination in restraint of trade, an employer's practices discriminatory, or a local governmental arrangement an abridgment of the right to vote on the basis of race or color—are far from obvious, and often have been sharply contested. And many of these principles, in turn, require a substantial and potentially controversial body of practical rules for their application. The Supreme Court and the federal judiciary it supervises have had to create substantial bodies of law whose origins are the compact and somewhat gnomic congressional utterances in these prominent legislative schemes.

This is not meant to be a complaint: On the contrary, the Sherman Antitrust Act, the Equal Employment Opportunities Act, and the Voting Rights Act figure among Congress's most important and successful enactments. They have facilitated a fruitful collaboration between Congress and the Supreme Court, in which the Court has treated Congress's broad normative stipulations as an invitation to give those stipulations attractive shape and workable detail. They do not, however, fit the command-response model of textual authority in which the textual utterance of the lawmaker is a command to be mechanically followed by the judiciary. They are clear instances in which the Supreme Court has been Congress's reflective partner, not its reflexive agent. One is tempted to say that these statutes have functioned like little constitutions—but that is exactly the point towards which we are working.

Before we turn back to the Constitution, let us consider the judicial role with regard to statutes of this sort—we might call them *foundational* statutes. The call these statutes make on the normative judgment of the judiciary does not flow from a lapse in draftsmanship or from the inevitable failure of statutory categories when their boundaries are put under pressure. Rather, they seem to represent a legislative strategy of generality and incompleteness. The doctrine which they have called forth, in turn, is constituted in important part by the independent normative judgment of the federal judiciary. It would be odd in the extreme for the Court to ask what Congress intended with regard to this or that case, when it is rather clear—even if we could get past the difficult idea of a large, bicameral assembly of political persons who have many different reasons for the casting of their votes having an intent—that Congress has formed no such intent. Instead, Congress has in effect put in place a broad legislative frame and invited (indeed, required) the judiciary to use its institutional resources over time and through a multiplicity of cases to develop a rich and detailed normative understanding of the area and a concomitant body of doctrine to implement that understanding. Congress's instruction in effect has been very general, on the order of "develop and maintain a body of law that best serves the goal of preventing inter-entity arrangements that retard rather than facilitate competition and trade." The particulars here are not important, and it may be that even this general formulation decides matters that the Sherman Antitrust Act should be understood to have left open for judicial reflection: It may be, for example, that the independent goal of preserving the capacity of small businesses to compete with massively large corporate entities is plausibly imputed to the Act. The important point is that there are few if any particulars, on the face of the Act or in the context of its enactment. Congress has set only the general terms of a broad partnership, in which the Court is obliged and empowered to do much of the normative work.

Some influential observers of legal process in the Anglo-American legal tradition see this as true of the enterprise of statutory interpretation in general. On their view, it is seldom if ever possible or desirable to find a subjective legislative "intent" to resolve those cases where text and context are open to reasonable competing interpretations. There are layers and layers of difficulty in pursuing the chimera of a literal legislative intent. We have, of course, what is at best radically imperfect information about the state of mind of any given legislator who voted for the measure which is to be construed. But let us suspend this obvious problem and imagine that legislative phenomenology is magically transparent. Now, in the mind of any given legislator who supported the legislation in question, we presumably will encounter a variety of incentives, commitments, strategies, and reflexes—some overlapping, some conflicting, and some too murky to characterize with any confidence—which net out (or which at the particular moment when the vote was taken netted out) to the impulse to vote in favor of the statute as it was worded. And in the midst of this dense morass we will find startling judgmental lacunae. So even confining ourselves to an individual legislator, and even imagining phenomenological transparency, it will be impossible to make plausible readings of actual intent about many important legislative details. Our troubles have just begun, of course; because now we have to speculate about the distribution of such fragmentary impulses—*intentoids*—among a sizable group of legislators. We have to impute a singular intent to a large body of variously imagined decision-makers, each of whom may well have had a variety of reasons for voting as he or she did; any two of whom may have had a different set of reasons from each other; and many of whom may have voted with an eye to political strategy or compromise motivated by concerns that had nothing to do with the specific matter at hand. In the end we could at best be driven to a counterfactual question of the form: "If Congress were to decide whether interpretation A or interpretation B better advanced the goals of this legislation, how would it answer?" That question, if treated seriously as a matter of fact, is highly speculative as it stands, of course; but even before we get to that problem, there are additional hurdles. If a substantial period of time has passed since the enactment of the statute before us, is the question of hypothetical decision properly addressed to the present legislature or the enacting legislature? And if, as seems likely, the enacting legislature is the proper addressee, are we to imagine the members of that body frozen in time, exposed only to that which they had then encountered, or instead, as having had their inaugural sensibilities and concerns modified by the experiences of our political community in the intervening years?[4]

Where does all this lead? Whatever judges may say about the enterprise of giving meaning to statutes about which there is room for reasonable disagreement, they simply cannot be responding to the literal intent of the enacting legislature; and further, it is far from clear that we would want them to do so if they could. What judges are and should be doing in the interpretive space left by a statute's text and context is constructing a meaning for the statute, making it an effective vehicle for the achievement of the purposes it is best understood to serve. In the vocabulary of our ongoing project of offering an account of our constitutional practices, judges in this view are invariably acting as the legislature's partners, not merely its agents.

I find this understanding of the judicial function with regard to the textual authority of legislation generally persuasive. But the important point for our purposes is a less heroic one: Whether or not judges who interpret statutes *invariably* find themselves acting as partners of the legislature, they certainly do on some occasions, most prominently with regard to what we have called foundational statutes, where it is clear that the legislature is expecting and depending upon the partnership of the judiciary. And there is no obvious reason why this is anything but positive, since it permits a fruitful collaboration in which the legislature is able to engage the front-line experience of the judiciary in the project of explicating the rules, or alternatively, to depend on the judiciary to save it from foolish mistakes.

Whatever else is true, the agency model, with its picture of legislative command/mechanical judicial response, does not enjoy the support of an unvarying judicial practice in the domain of ordinary legislation. *If* there is a pervasive model of the way in which judges in the Anglo-American tradition connect to statutes, it is a model of partnership, not agency. At the very least, partnership is prominently characteristic of the role of the judiciary with regard to some very important and esteemed legislative schemes. Originalists, accordingly, cannot help themselves to a general model of textual authority. They must defend their strict protocol with regard to the distinct question of the Constitution's textual authority.

The Constitution

The enacted Constitution offers originalists very poor ground on which to mount their defense. The liberty-bearing provisions of the Constitution typically speak at a high level of generality, and can only sensibly be understood as invoking broad principles of political justice that require a great deal of elaboration before they can produce concrete results in actual controversies. Consider three well-traveled and much-esteemed provisions: the First Amendment's commitment to "freedom of speech," the two clauses in the same Amendment that combine to protect religious liberty, and the Fourteenth

Amendment's guarantee of "equal protection of the laws." Between them these provisions are the textual predicate of much of the modern jurisprudence of constitutional justice. But free speech, religious liberty, and equal protection are very general ideas, ideas whose basic thrust and practical extension have been the source of much disagreement. The First Amendment seems to speak plainly: "Congress shall make no law . . . abridging freedom of speech." And Justice Hugo Black famously purported to believe that these words standing alone offered clear guidance through the labyrinth of issues confronted by the Supreme Court in pursuit of free expression.[5] But, in fact, the modern Court has had to work out a complex scheme for the protection of speech, full of subtle and not so subtle distinctions that have depended on a wide range of normative judgments, based in turn on questions of value, institutional competence, and the understanding of unfolding judicial precedent. The Constitution's text and historical context provide an important starting point, and a kind of rhetorical affirmation of the Court's robust commitment to free expression, but they simply cannot answer the hard questions with which the Court has had to deal. Consider speech that has the aim (and possibly the tendency) of subverting the very constitutional order which is being invoked to protect it. Is such subversive advocacy (a) a despised outcast and enemy of the Constitution, vulnerable in whole or in part to legislative perceptions of a threat to the well-being of our political community; or (b) highly protected precisely because it is exquisitely political speech, and subject to regulation only under extreme circumstances where speech and action are brought so close together as to make the speech in effect part of the subversive act? Or consider pornography and racially directed hate speech. Is the prohibition of these forms of speech (a) justified under some circumstances because of the tendency of such speech to make the vulnerable still more vulnerable; or (b) singularly disfavored, because it targets speech because of its message? Or consider the public burning of the flag as a means of protest. Is the symbolic value of the flag, its status as cultural property (a) a good reason for making its desecration illegal; or (b) precisely why its expressive destruction must be protected?

The picture with regard to religious liberty is no better from the vantage of the dig into history proffered by originalism as the means of assigning content to the Constitution. The First Amendment devotes much of its sparse language to this theme: "Congress shall make no law respecting an establishment of religion, or prohibiting the free exercise thereof. . . ." Very basic questions survive the text and its historical context, however. For example: Does the Constitution merely offer religious believers protection from discrimination and the benefits of personal liberties available to all, or does it go further, and privilege religious believers against the imposition of otherwise valid laws of general application which interfere with the requirements of their faith? Are religious enterprises constitutionally entitled to participate on equal terms with secular ones in governmentally funded programs, or does the Constitution debar governments from permitting religious enterprises to be the beneficiaries of public funds and services? Similarly, where and on what rationale is the line to be drawn between the impermissible incorporation of religious exercises in public schools and universities, on the one hand, and the mandate that public fora within such entities treat all expression including religious expression equally?

Constitutional equality has only a sparse textual reference as its starting point—the Fourteenth Amendment declares that "No State shall . . . deny to any person within its jurisdiction the equal protection of the laws." But it has the pointed and poignant historical context of the Civil War and its Reconstruction aftermath. The net result is no different for our purposes; here, too, fundamental questions of constitutional meaning arise, questions which require for their resolution more than the originalist protocol can offer. Are the exclusive beneficiaries of constitutional equality the African-American slaves who were emancipated by the Civil War and its aftermath, or are other groups or individuals also entitled to "equal protection of the laws"? What qualifies a group or an individual for judicial protection against discrimination in the name of the Constitution, and, in particular, do women as a group qualify for such protection? When, if ever, are separate facilities for Caucasians and African-Americans, or men and women, consistent with constitutional equality? Are programs which single out racial minorities or other vulnerable groups for benefits rather than burdens constitutionally suspect, and, more generally, under what circumstances should such programs be understood to be inconsistent with the requirements of constitutional equality?

This rendition of constitutional uncertainty is, of course, woefully undernourished. I have gestured towards only a few of the deep questions of meaning that these three staples of our constitutional jurisprudence pose, and suggested only a few of the possible responses to those questions. In the actual world of constitutional adjudication there has been and must be a level of nuance, detail, and complexity to which a brief summary like this cannot possibly do justice. And we have been considering relatively concrete and mature aspects of our constitutional tradition. Other very important areas—like the substantive guarantee of independence we attach to the due process clauses, and the boundaries of the overlapping authority of the three branches of the federal government—pose questions which are at least as elusive of historical reconstruction as these. But these observations, of course, merely strengthen my point: No satisfactory approach to the Constitution can stop at the excavation of history that originalist theorists insist is the dominant if not exclusive source of constitutional meaning accessible to judges. With apologies to the memory of Justice Black, no one, I think, will argue that the text of these three clauses can answer any—

let alone all—of the questions we have sketched. The text of the Constitution is not an adequate guide to questions of constitutional meaning at the level of concrete detail.

If this is not obvious from our catalog of major questions confronting the Court in speech, religion, and equal protection cases, consider a narrower list, offered by Justice Antonin Scalia.[6] Justice Scalia means this list to be a sharp criticism of his colleagues, who he thinks have deserted the text and gone off on an illegitimate normative adventure on their own. Worse, they have shackled democratic government in myriad ways; Scalia's list is of the things that popular political institutions were once permitted to do, and now cannot. For Scalia they all represent judicial mistakes—mistakes that a judge who only permitted herself to be guided by the Constitution's text would not make:

- admitting in a state criminal trial evidence of guilt that was obtained by an unlawful search;
- permitting invocation of God at public-school graduations;
- electing one of the two houses of a state legislature the way the United States Senate is elected, i.e., on a basis that does not give all voters numerically equal representation;
- terminating welfare payments as soon as evidence of fraud is received, subject to restoration after hearing if the evidence is satisfactorily refuted;
- imposing property requirements as a condition of voting;
- prohibiting anonymous campaign literature;
- prohibiting pornography.

But this is a curious list for Justice Scalia to have offered as a means of persuading us that the Constitution's text has been ignored by the modern constitutional judiciary. The Fourth Amendment, after all, clearly makes a range of police search practices unconstitutional: Can/should/must the constitutional judiciary devise mechanisms like the exclusionary rule which punish unconstitutional police practices and bar state and federal judges from involving themselves with the fruits of those practice? The First Amendment emphatically protects the "free exercise of religion," and bars the "establishment" of religion: Are publicly endorsed prayer rituals offensive to the vision of religious liberty that underlies these prohibitions? The liberty-bearing provisions of the Constitution concern themselves more with the right to vote than with any other theme, and they include, of course, the guarantee of constitutional equality contained in the Equal Protection Clause: Did the radically disparate voting strengths of voters in the rural parts of many states as opposed to those in the urban parts of those states violate the Constitution's pervasive and textually represented demand for a fair distribution of the franchise? And further, does putting a price on the opportunity to vote violate the fair distribution of the franchise? Everyone agrees that the due process clauses of the Fifth and Fourteenth Amendments require fair procedures when the government is dealing with crucial aspects of people's lives, and that hearings are often essential to fair procedures: When government thinks it may have a reason for depriving a person of payments crucial to his subsistence, must it first give him a hearing at which he can offer evidence to rebut that reason? The Constitution's textual commitment to freedom of expression is perfectly clear: No one doubts that political speech is at the heart of the First Amendment's concerns; does a state restriction on anonymous campaign literature do violence to that commitment? And further, is the regulation of films, magazines, or books because of the way they portray women or men as the objects of sexual gratification or because of the explicitness of their portrayal of sexual activity inconsistent with the First Amendment?

None of these questions has a perfectly obvious answer, and it is entirely possible that Justice Scalia and I would disagree about the right answers to many of them. But the important point is that each of these questions arises in the context of a constitutional controversy that can fairly be described as follows: In each case, individuals or groups object to a harm that they have suffered or will suffer as a result of a governmental decision; in each, there is a textually plausible claim that the offending decision violates the Constitution; and in each, the text undeniably stops short of insisting that the claim is valid. In short, the text and widely acknowledged context of the Constitution put every one of these questions on a fair-minded judge's agenda; but standing alone, text and context resolve none of them.

CHAPTER 3

Enactment-Centered History as an Originalist Supplementation of the Text

In the face of the limited guidance provided by the Constitution's text, how can originalists persevere? The most common strategy is to supplement the text of the Constitution with some other enactment-centered resource. Surely originalists are right in encouraging interpreters of the Constitution to view its formal text in the context of the circumstances surrounding its adoption. Reading the Equal Protection Clause in isolation from the Civil War and Reconstruction's attempt to purge our political community not just of the moral scandal of slavery but of its durable cultural consequences would be a great mistake; and any attractive understanding of constitutional equality will have this context as its point of departure. But nothing in that history answers any of the hard questions about constitutional equality; and the picture is no better elsewhere in the liberty-bearing precincts of the Constitution. This becomes increasingly clear as we consider the sorts of resources that originalists offer to supplement the Constitution's text.

One such resource is suggested by Robert Bork. All that counts, Bork insists, "is how the words used in the Constitution would have been understood *at the time*."[1] Even this blunt use of words is a little unclear, as it happens. Bork could have in mind, in effect, a time-specific, law-drenched dictionary from which the meaning of—to continue our example—the Fourteenth Amendment's stipulation that "[n]o State shall . . . deny to any person within its jurisdiction the equal protection of the laws" could be read; or he might have in mind the more complex idea that we can infer from various historical circumstances surrounding the drafting and ratification of the Fourteenth Amendment something more decisive about the collective state of mind of the enacting generation. For the moment, it is the first of these possibilities, the dictionary, that I want to put on the table.

Some words do change their meaning over time. In particular, words may vary dramatically in their capaciousness. At one time, the meaning of *sanction* included permission or approval; now it is used almost exclusively to describe a punishment for a delict. Until recently, *weather* was a generic invocation of the meteorological state of affairs; now it is often used to mean blustery, bad . . . well, weather. *Attitude* has undergone a similar foreshortening in some quarters, though I have the sense that is used to describe a particular form of bad attitude with considerable approval.[2]

If words or phrases in the Constitution have undergone this sort of change of meaning, judges should certainly know about it, and follow the original meaning of the word. There may well be such cases. The President, for example, can be impeached only for "high crimes or misdemeanors." Today, "misdemeanor" is immediately understood as a formal reference to a comparatively petty criminal offense. In 1787, the original meaning of "misdemeanor" as a less formal reference to seriously bad conduct—mis-demeanor—was very much in vogue. Even if the problem is not temporal but just an enduring quirk of the English language, judges clearly should determine what the intended meaning was, and follow it. If *sanction* had always had diametric meanings, and if it were used in the Constitution, judges should try to determine which meaning was intended—

it would probably be pretty obvious—and they should follow that meaning, not the one they thought would make the Constitution a better constitution. So understood, the mandate to understand the text of the Constitution as it would have been understood at the time of its enactment is unobjectionable.

But this is of little or no help to the originalist. Consider the range of questions I offered as crucial to the shape of modern understandings of the constitutional status of speech, religion, and equal protection. Few if any of these questions—and certainly none of those which are live issues for the modern Court—turn on confusion about the dictionary meaning of the constitutional language. There is in fact, broad agreement about the meaning of the relevant words of the Constitution. If the reader has any doubts about the typicality of my list, she can substitute Justice Scalia's, where once again the dictionary will be of very little use. And if any doubts of this kind still remain, I invite the reader to substitute her favorite constitutional controversy. The resources of a time-specific, law-drenched dictionary are simply no great help to the constitutional decision-maker, and hence no great help to the originalist, who bears at least the burden of satisfying us that the originalist protocol can go some substantial distance towards actually deciding cases.

Some originalists would see the failure of the time-specific dictionary as beside the point. When they argue that we should give the text of the Constitution the meaning it had at the time of its enactment, they mean to supplement the text with more than the immediate historical context of its enactment, and more than a dictionary. They claim that constitutional judges should interpret the text in light of what the framers had in mind as entailed by the text. This general characterization does not fully elucidate the originalists' assertion, in part because it may not have a stable or coherent form. We can best do justice to their claim by considering examples of the sort that they seem to have in mind, and then by trying to understand the general point these examples illustrate.

One example is the connection between the possibility that capital punishment violates the Eighth Amendment's prohibition of cruel and unusual punishment, juxtaposed with the stipulations in the Fifth and Fourteenth Amendments that no person shall be deprived of "life . . . without due process of law," and the further stipulation in the Fifth Amendment that no person should be held to answer for a capital crime absent an indictment by a grand jury. A second example is the connection between the renunciation in *Brown v. Board of Education*[3] of "separate but equal" public schools, and the fact that at the time of the enactment of the Fourteenth Amendment—and for nearly three-quarters of a century thereafter—the racially segregated schools of the District of Columbia were largely unchallenged. A third example—in the same conceptual spirit, but from the other side of the aisle—is the acceptance of some forms of affirmative racial preferences in the period surrounding the birth of the Fourteenth Amendment.

What these examples have in common is in a certain sense easy to state: Each involves a constitutional premise (racially segregated schools violate the Equal Protection Clause) coupled with some evidence to the effect that members of the generation that enacted the pertinent portion of the Constitution did not think that the premise in question was an entailment of their enactment (the maintenance of segregated schools in the District of Columbia). For the originalist, the general idea is that the text has been thickened by the contemporary evidence of how it was understood by the framing generation.

It is very seldom the case that the answers to important constitutional questions are reflected in a stable, widespread understanding by the framing generation of the entailments of the text they are enacting. In this respect, capital punishment is a special, possibly unique case, since there is collateral constitutional text available to buttress the belief that the framing generation did not think that all forms of capital punishment were cruel and unusual within the meaning of the Eighth Amendment.[4] When we turn elsewhere, the prospect for originalist reconstruction of this sort is much bleaker.[5] As to the phenomenology of the framing generation as a whole, we of course have no reliable information.

Or consider the area of religious liberty, about which the framing generation was quite self-conscious and articulate. Included in our earlier list of constitutional issues that outrun any possibility of textual resolution was a choice between two quite different understandings of the Constitution's commitment to religious liberty. The Constitution might treat religion as an especially valuable human activity which ought to be permitted to flourish even at the sacrifice of other legitimate and substantial concerns of the state; or the Constitution might treat religion as especially vulnerable to discrimination and set out to prevent religious believers from being treated with less than equal regard.[6] Even a complete historical record of the framers' intentions on these matters (assuming, *arguendo*, that this were epistemologically possible) would leave us with a choice between these fundamentally different understandings of religious liberty.[7] It bears emphasis that school segregation and the fundamental structure of religious liberty are instances where the historical record is comparatively dense and the promise of the originalist protocol comparatively high. The prospects for enactment-centered history in most other contexts are, if anything, far worse.

This is just the beginning of the difficulty for an originalist who appeals to the understandings of the framing generation. Suppose we find a case where we are reasonably confident that among the framing generation there was a widely shared understanding of the enacted text. Let us suppose, for example, that among the political generation that ratified the Fourteenth Amendment there was a widely shared belief that segregated education was consistent with the Amendment's demand for equal protection of the laws. Further, suppose for the moment that a justice of the Supreme Court in *Brown v. Board of Education* were tempted to give this understanding the force of law. Our hypothetical originalist justice would find herself in a pickle.

To understand the problem, consider the story of an old political activist, and his young, much-devoted protégé.[8] On many occasions, including their last time together, the old activist would insist that no society was just in which persons willing to work hard were unable to provide the necessities of a minimally decent material life for themselves and their families. He would also insist that only a political community with a deeply collectivized economy could ever secure this critical element of justice for its members. At the funeral of his friend, the young protégé vows to devote his life "to the ideals and commitments of the man I admire most." Later, the now not so young protégé has become an important, crusading political figure. He has also come to the clear belief that his political community can come much closer to realizing the ideal of guaranteed minimum welfare for all with a market economy than with a collectivized one.

Consider the protégé's situation: The problem is not just that he has come to disagree with his mentor's view about the virtues of a collectivized economy. He may be no less firm in his resolve to model his life on the ideals and commitments of his mentor, come what may; but some of those, he now understands, are antagonistic to each other. He cannot work both to collectivize the economy and to secure minimum welfare for all, because to accomplish the one is to undermine the other. He has to choose, and if he is at all sensible, he will jettison the goal of a collectivized economy. He wants to make his community better, not worse; and he wants to realize his mentor's vision of a society in which no one lacks the ingredients of a materially decent life. It would be perverse for the protégé to pursue his mentor's mistake at the cost of his mentor's dream.

We embarked on this story as a means of illustrating the plight of a justice of the Supreme Court who was inclined to an originalist protocol of adjudication and believed that there was widespread sympathy for segregated schools among the Fourteenth Amendment's framing generation when she tried to reach a decision in *Brown v. Board of Education*. On any plausible reading, the Equal Protection Clause insists that African-Americans enjoy the status of equal members of our political community; and to our hypothetical justice it should have been obvious (even in 1954) that the highly visible maintenance of Jim Crow separatism was radically inconsistent with equal membership. It thus would be impossible for our justice to be faithful both to the ideal of constitutional equality and to the view of the framing generation that segregated schools were consistent with constitutional equality. She would have to choose, just as the activist protégé had to choose; and, just as in the case of the activist protégé, it would be perverse to choose away from racial equality in favor of the framing generation's mistake about the relationship between segregated public schools and that core ideal of the Fourteenth Amendment. It would be perverse precisely to the enterprise of maintaining fidelity to the Equal Protection Clause.

How might originalists who want in this way to supplement the general moral commitments of the Constitution respond? They might claim something like this: Widely shared understandings of the framing generation as to the application of the moral principles of the Constitution are as much a part of the meaning of the Constitution's instructions as the widely shared understanding that, say, the Impeachment Clause refers to misdemeanors in the sense of gravely bad acts generally, not in the modern sense of low-level crimes. Further, they might argue, the more particular elements of the framing generation's understanding should dominate, just as with a statute that includes both general terms and a definitional section which includes or excludes particular cases from the ambit of those terms. Such widely shared understandings, in effect, are to be regarded as more-detailed material in the historical dictionary that tells us what the generation that drafted and ratified the provisions of the Constitution had in mind.

But this ignores the important distinction between what an instruction requires of those who set out to follow it and what the author of the instruction expects to be the outcome of her instruction being faithfully followed.[9] The existence of such a distinction is obvious: If the dean of a law school tells a constitutional law professor that she is to designate the student who wrote the best examination in her class to receive a prize at graduation, the professor's faithful execution of that instruction might well upset the expectations of the dean. The dean may know that *X,* the reigning wunderkind, is in the class and confidently expect (perhaps even hope) that *X* will win the prize; but the teacher correctly understands the instruction to be "Designate the student who in your careful judgment wrote the best examination," not "Designate the student who I anticipate will be deemed by you to have written the best examination." And this would be so even if out of curiosity the dean asks to read the best ten examinations and thinks that in fact *X* wrote by far the best examination. The instruction, we assume, is still meant to be "Designate the student who in your careful judgment wrote the best examination," not "Designate the student who I think wrote the best examination."[10] It is true, of course, that when we consult the law-drenched history-sensitive dictionary to determine the meaning of "misdemeanor" in the impeachment clause, we are inquiring into the shared linguistic understanding or practice of the framing generation, but that inquiry does not conceptually unravel the Constitution's words to leave us with the threads of the framing generation's shared expectations as to the outcomes of their constitutional commitments. The instruction that "the President should be impeached only upon a finding that he has committed an act so bad as to justify his removal from office" is fundamentally different than the instruction that "the President should be impeached only upon a finding that he has committed an act that we in the framing generation would believe is so bad as to justify his removal from office."

So it is a confusion to think that all pertinent matters about which the framing generation might have shared a general consensus are necessarily part of the meaning of the textual instructions they gave in the Constitution—part of the history-drenched dictionary which must be consulted in reading the Constitution. Their understanding of what the words they used meant is important; but that understanding need not be seen to include their expectations about the application of their words to actual legal decisions in the future. I say "need not," because to observe the important distinction between the meaning of an instruction and the expectations of the instruction's author is to raise, not to conclude, the question of whether the meaning of the Constitution's instructions should be taken to include widely shared expectations of the framing generation. If it is true, for example, that the framing generation generally believed that segregated schools were compatible with racial equality, it remains to be determined whether that belief should be treated as part of their instruction, or merely as an expectation (happily, a mistaken expectation) of what would happen when their instruction was followed.

What should be the grounds upon which we make that determination? There are at least three possibilities: We could look to the intention of a given framing generation itself, and hope to find a consensus among that diffuse group as to the legal status of some or all of its nontextualized expectations; we could consult the practice of textualized lawmaking, and seek an account of that practice that helps to determine when if ever the nontextualized expectations of lawmakers should be considered to be part of the instructions they author; or we could look to our constitutional practice itself, asking whether including or excluding expectations of the framing generation as to constitutional outcomes better captures and/or justifies that practice. These possible arbiters of the status of the framing generation's expectations could be connected to each other in various ways as well. For example, we could think that there was an arbitral ladder such that the interpretive intentions of the framing generation should govern if there was in fact a widely shared interpretive consensus; that failing such a consensus we should look next to the practice of textualized lawmaking; and that only failing answers there should we look to our constitutional practice itself. Or we could invert the ladder. Or we could see more contingent connections among these arbiters: It seems natural, for example, to read the interpretive intentions of the framing generation against the backdrop of our practice of textualized lawmaking in general and our constitutional practice in particular.

These are interesting questions, but they need not detain us here, because whichever of these arbiters we consult points away from treating the expectations of the framing generation as part of their constitutional instructions. Consider what sense we can make of the interpretive intentions of the generations that framed the Constitution and its amendments: Most of the liberty-bearing provisions of the Constitution speak at a high level of generality and invoke lofty and rather abstract ideals, like equal protection, due process, freedom of expression, and the free exercise of religion. Yet, when the framers wanted to, they could descend to the particular, as with the Seventh Amendment's provision for jury trials in civil matters where the amount in controversy exceeds twenty dollars. (It is not accidental that particularized provisions like this one are among the Constitution's least successful—but that points us towards another arbiter, of course.) If we could with any confidence assign an understanding to the Constitution's framing generations of the status of their expectations, it would surely be one which respected the open texture of most of the relevant constitutional text rather than drastically more particular, textually suppressed expectations of specific outcomes.

And what of the best account of textualized lawmaking? Here, there may be somewhat more room for disagreement; but increasingly, reflective theorists of statutory interpretation are coming to the view that honest textual ambiguity seldom if ever can or should be resolved by reference to the subjective intent of the lawmaking body. In chapter 2 we noted that some of the most important provisions in federal law—we characterized them as "foundational" provisions—are framed at a level of generality that has required and received the independent normative judgment of the judiciary in fashioning a workable body of law; further, we noted that this was a sensible and attractive legislative strategy of partnership. There may or may not be grounds for concluding that nontextualized expectations of outcome are pervasively denied authority under the best account of textualized lawmaking; but this is surely true of the subdepartment of the practice of textualized lawmaking that is most like constitutional law. The situation, emphatically, is not like a statute that explicitly modifies its general terms with more specific provisos. Here, the Constitution's text speaks at a notably high level of generality, all but insisting upon the reflective judgment of those who commit themselves to constitutional fidelity, and it is the tacit expectations of members of the framing generation that are being invoked to frustrate that judgment.

My own instincts strongly favor consulting the practice of constitutional law itself. Remember how we came to the present inquiry: We began by considering the situation that confronts a judge who believes—ignoring for the moment evidence of a contrary consensus among the members of the relevant framing generation—that segregated public schools are at drastic odds with the equal protection clause's guarantee of racial equality, or that capital punishment violates the Eighth Amendment's prohibition of cruel and unusual punishment. Now we imagine that the judge is an originalist, who treats as authoritative the widely held expectations of the framing generation. Further, we assume that these two cases are exceptional, in that there really is a widely held expectation to be recovered, and that in each instance that expectation is contrary to the judge's view of the underlying constitutional value at stake. Such a judge, we noted, would be under conflicting instructions from the framing generation and would have to elect between them. Now, it is precisely from the vantage of making sense of our constitutional practice overall that it seems so odd—indeed, perverse—to imagine that the judge should choose away from the fundamental constitutional value of constitutional equality or constitutional humanity in favor of what she can only understand as a mistake of the framing generation in applying that value to specific cases.

What could possibly be said on behalf of requiring constitutional judges to act in this apparently perverse way? Presumably, the defender of originalism will take something like the following line: Most modern constitutional decisions of any real importance are contestable and indeed are contested; there is the real possibility of reasonable disagreement, and further the real possibility of error. So, while it may seem obvious to a given judge or court what the right decision is, we are better off from the standpoint of constitutional justice if we keep the independent normative judgment of contemporary judges out of the picture and rely on the enacted Constitution, including widely held and well-settled expectations of the relevant framing generation as to the outcome of the Constitution they enacted. Better off, that is, in one or both of two possible ways. First, we'll get better outcomes; and second, we'll get outcomes that are more consistent with democracy—more consistent, that is, with the fair distribution of political authority.

The question of whether we have reason to expect good outcomes from a constitutional judiciary that acts as the partner rather
than the agent of the framing generations and the further question
of whether a judiciary that behaves in this way is consistent with
democracy will occupy much of our attention in the pages that
follow. But, for the moment, we are concerned with a narrower
issue, namely, whether we make our constitutional practice more
efficacious or more democratic by binding judges to widely held
expectations among the framing generations as to the concrete outcomes of the faithful application of the broad principles of the
liberty-bearing provisions they enacted into the Constitution.

When we think about moral progress under our Constitution, it
seems highly improbable that letting the settled expectations of the
framers govern would increase our conformity with the fundamental precepts of political justice. As augmented by the Bill of Rights,
the original Constitution had two great defects: It tolerated the morally grotesque practice of slavery, and it exempted state and local
governments from the reach of most of its liberty-bearing provisions. Reconstruction and its aftermath went a considerable distance
to correcting those defects, and left us with a workable—and in the
main attractive—structure of constitutional justice. After Reconstruction at least, our worst constitutional failings have consisted of
asking the right questions and getting the wrong answers, of naming
the right moral ideals but lacking the courage or moral imagination
to give those ideals their full reach. Consider, for example, our toler-
ation of Jim Crow laws and the exclusion of women from work and
independent wealth.

The following hypothesis seems plausible, in light of our actual
experience as a political community—and I suspect, in light of many
of our experiences in our personal lives: It is easier to commit ourselves to sound moral principles at a comparatively abstract level
than it is to live out those commitments in our day-to-day lives,

when we have to pay the costs associated with the commitments. Moral progress, accordingly, is often associated with broad forward reaches of principle, followed by much slower and more halting progress on the level of the concrete. In time, our moral imaginations and moral achievements grow to fill more of our aspirations, and the unthinkable becomes the normal and seemingly inevitable adjustment of our affairs to meet our obligations and commitments. This is increasingly true, for example, of the laggard recognition of African-Americans as richly endowed, fully entitled members of our political community; and of the comparable recognition of women as equals of men in every reach of our public and private lives. Sometimes, this characteristic disparity between our own ideals and our concrete applications is contained in a single person or a single moment. Thomas Jefferson's complex, tortuous (and possibly tortured) relationship to the institution of slavery is one such example. Hugo Black's opinion in *Korematsu* is another.[11] What a sad and grotesque irony: to have the first articulate announcement of the deep suspicion with which our Constitution views racial scapegoating appear in an opinion upholding the herding of loyal Japanese-Americans into detention camps.

We have a tendency, thus, to fall short in practice not only of what we preach, but of what we actually believe and take on board as a principle which we should respect in the conduct of our political affairs. That tendency would be especially pronounced in our constitutional practice were we to treat the expectations of the members of the framing generations as authority that controlled our interpretation of their textual commitments. This would be true for two reasons. First, the expectations of the framing generation are functionally stale. They were formed under demographic, cultural, and geopolitical circumstances very different than those that prevail today; and they were formed without the benefit of decades or even centuries of our experience as a political community committed to the ideals of the Constitution. They are thus singularly bad sources of guidance. Second, our process of constitution-making has practical features that make it reasonably well suited to the articulation of principles worthy of our concern and commitment; but those pragmatic virtues attach to what the framing generation made into law, not to the expectations among that generation as to how that law would come to be applied to specific cases. After all, what was inscribed into the law—drafted and redrafted, worried about and debated at length, and ultimately voted out of one deliberative body after another until the formalities of ratification were satisfied—was the Constitution's text. That is what survived public scrutiny and, at least as a functional matter, satisfied the burden of public justification. "No state shall deprive its citizens . . . of the equal protection of the laws" was debated and ratified; not "Racially segregated schools are consistent with the demands of equal protection."

The point, ultimately, is this: What we hope to get from our constitutional practice as a whole is a strong prod towards conformity with the fundamentals of political justice. Set against that goal, it seems perverse to let even widely shared expectations among members of the relevant framing generation about the application of constitutional ideals dominate our best contemporary judgment about the application of those ideals.

Given that the expectation-driven version of originalism would generate a constitutional practice poorly suited to sound results, there remains only a procedural defense of this proposed protocol, a defense based on democracy. The idea would be that the fair distribution of political authority requires that political majorities rather than the constitutional judiciary make important decisions for our political community, and that, accordingly, contestable questions of constitutional application should be referred to the judgment of the framing generation.

Claims on behalf of originalism that invoke democracy suffer from a common problem: They depend upon a political consensus among persons who have long since departed from our political community. We will defer a general discussion of the implications of this blunt fact until we take up the broader question of democracy and constitutional adjudication. But, for our present purposes, it is useful to note that originalist attempts to convert the expectations of the framing generation into legal commands are particularly lame from the perspective of democracy. We have already noted that—to the extent that we can infer anything about the collective state of mind or intent of a political generation that helped to frame the Constitution—the Constitution's framers intended to create the legal commands they reduced to text, not a set of commands based upon their expectations as to outcomes under those textual commands. So the originalist of this variety is seeking to revive a long since stale judgment of a political generation that never intended to enact that judgment into law, in a time and a place and in light of durable experience that might well have persuaded that very generation to revise its view. Surely democracy does not encourage us to do any such thing.

This completes our excursion into the question of whether widely shared expectations of the Constitution's framers should be given legal authority as though they were part of the Constitution's instructions. Our answer has been an emphatic no. But the length of our excursion should not distract us from the important observation with which we began: There will seldom if ever be occasions on which we could say with any confidence at all that the Constitution's framers in fact had such shared expectations. If the Constitution's text and context do not point us to a single outcome (and we have seen that they almost always do not), the originalist protocol will fail for the most mundane of reasons: It cannot offer answers to the questions with which modern constitutional law is preoccupied.

CHAPTER 4

Three Rescue Attempts:
Lean, Middling, and Thick

Before we turn to partnership accounts of the Constitution, we should consider attempts to rescue the agency account of the obligation of a constitutional judge. The first of these we might characterize as *parsimonious* originalism.

A Parsimonious Originalist Constitution

We have been at pains to support the observation that the Constitution's text and its enactment-centered history simply cannot resolve most modern controversies. An originalist might see this as a false or shallow complaint. To the true originalist, the chips fall from an enactment-centered history where they may: If the text and context of the Constitution do not produce unequivocal answers to any given problem, then that is the best of reasons to keep the Constitution out of the picture, and let the ordinary mechanisms of popular debate and popular politics operate unimpeded by contestable readings of the Constitution.

Interestingly, to my knowledge, no prominent originalist theorist is actually able to live within the narrow strictures of the originalist protocol once it is described in this way. Robert Bork, for example, abandons the narrow base of decisional resources offered by originalism when the moment arrives to describe the boundaries of what is and what is not protected speech; then he rolls up his normative sleeves and starts arguing for what he regards as a sound and sensible version of the First Amendment. More remarkably, Bork argues at length for restrictions on affirmative action in the name of the Fourteenth Amendment, without offering a single non-contestable originalist resource in support of his position. Justice Antonin Scalia presents much the same profile: He has been a staunch supporter of the Supreme Court's decisions imposing substantial constitutional restrictions on affirmative action and on race-conscious electoral districting, without an originalist leg to stand on. And, in at least two other constitutional areas, he has successfully sponsored sophisticated and controversial extensions of the Constitution's reach that are notably lacking in the untroubled historical pedigree required by pure originalism. He has more or less single-handedly crafted a new federal jurisprudence of the rights of the owners of real property against regulatory depredations, and he has been conceptually nimble in defense of a broad conception of free expression, a conception which leaves little if any room for restrictions on hate speech.

All of these doctrinal maneuverings, it must be remembered, assume what is now unquestioned and crucial in our constitutional jurisprudence: that the states are bound in full by most of the provisions of the Bill of Rights. That proposition itself is almost certainly out of the reach of the pure originalist. Even *Brown v. Board of Education* is beyond the originalist pale; the most pro-*Brown* revisionist history, on fair reading, merely puts us in the same limbo of constitutional uncertainty to which originalism assigns the answer to every interesting and important constitutional question.

The point, of course, is not that current originalist heroes happen to have conceptual feet of clay. The point is that originalist theorists are not describing our constitutional practice as it even remotely is or has been; they are not describing our practice as it should be, because their recipe would reduce the majestic commands of the Constitution to a lean and unuseful residue of what is clear beyond all doubt; they are not even describing our practice as they actually wish it to be. If fidelity to the Constitution really required this degree of parsimony, then no one faithful to the Constitution could be fidelity's friend. And if an honest originalist came on the scene he or she would be welcomed by almost no one.

Modest Originalism

This leaves one wondering, of course, exactly what originalists can imagine themselves to be doing when they participate in modern constitutional discourse. One possibility is what we might think of as modest originalism. Michael McConnell offers one version of this when he describes two different originalist ways of supplementing the bare text. First, we could read the Constitution "in light of the Framers' expectations about specific applications"; this, as we have seen, is not a plausible conceptual option, and McConnell agrees. Second, we could read the Constitution in light of "the moral and political principles [the framers] intended to express." This possibility, McConnell believes, can rescue originalism.[1]

So put, McConnell's prescription for modest originalism is ambiguous between two possible instructions for constitutional judges. On the first reading, judges would be confined to the enactment-centered resources of strict originalism, but here the Constitution's text would be supplemented not by the framers' tacit specific expectations, but rather by the "moral and political principles" they intended to express. On the second reading, judges would not be confined in a recognizably originalist way at all: They would be expected to bring substantial normative resources of their own to the process of judgment, as in the partnership account of constitutional judging, but they would in some sense be limited by the principles of the framers (or more sensibly, the framing generation).

The first reading offers no help to originalism. Uncontroversial explications of the "moral and political principles" that the framers intended to express in the liberty-bearing provisions of the Constitution are surely available. But as before, they are at best starting points for judgment: Freedom of speech, freedom of religion, and equal membership in our political community are all moral and political principles that the framers intended to express and succeeded in expressing; but they cannot decide cases without being imbued with exactly the sort of normative detail that is not available and that would not be a conceptually attractive grounds for decision if it were.

What could McConnell have in mind? He offers two examples—really one example with two variations: First, he imagines that the framing generation thought that "any procedure that had been used by the states for a great period of time was 'due process'"; and second, he imagines that due process (or better, the Privileges and Immunities Clause) has a substantive aspect, but that it too "was understood by the framers of the Fourteenth Amendment to protect rights that had been protected by most of the states for a significant period of time."

These are interesting and subtle cases for McConnell to put on the table in the name of his modest originalism. Textually, "due process" and "privileges and immunities" are plausible candidates for the reading that McConnell suggests might be best. Both phrases can sensibly be read as intending to restrain state conduct that deviates widely from the accepted norm. But, even taken at face value for the moment, this is a claim that can do very little to help originalism. What, for example, of "freedom of speech," "free exercise of religion," and "equal protection"? Here, at the heart of the liberty-bearing provisions of the Constitution, there is no comparably plausible reading that narrows the normative work that must be done by responsible constitutional interpreters.

So McConnell can only be defending the second reading of his claim—namely that judges will have to act in a distinctly nonoriginalist way most of the time, but should respect what he believes to be better readings of what the framing generation "intended to express" in those few clauses that are fairly open to being read as historical or inertial rather than as direct statements of substantive principle. Even as to these clauses, McConnell has an impossibly steep upward slope to negotiate. Consider the conceptually distinct possible readings to which his hypothesized reading of these clauses is open. First, there is the divide between the idea that the Fourteenth Amendment incorporates by reference a fixed set of rights that were widely recognized by most states at the time of the ratification of the Fourteenth Amendment, on the one hand; and the idea that the Fourteenth Amendment prohibits deviations from currently well-established national norms, on the other. Second, there is the possibility that what the framing generation "meant to express" were indeed substantive principles of the sort that are characteristic of the other liberty-bearing provisions of the Constitution, but that they imagined either that those rights, then widely recognized, were largely exhaustive of those principles; or alternatively, they expected that well-established national norms would at any given time be the preferred starting point for analysis of the demands of those principles. The idea that a suitably deep dig into the history of the Fourteenth Amendment is going to yield convincing evidence that selects among these possible readings is radically implausible. McConnell himself, for example, is a competent, energetic, and tendentious constitutional historian, and his efforts to date—including his revisionist history of the Fourteenth Amendment—have failed to yield data remotely approaching what would be required to make a case on historical grounds for interpretations of the sort he proposes to assign to the Due Process Clause or the Privileges and Immunities Clause.

Reluctant Judgment Theory

There is a third possible response to the problems of originalism to consider, one which in all probability would not be welcomed by most originalists. As we noted earlier, one theme in the scholarly conversation about our constitutional practice is this: A conscientious judge, setting out to be as faithful as possible to the instructions of the Constitution (and/or whatever other instructions are taken to be binding upon her) will discover that what we might call pure or simple fidelity to the Constitution's instructions is impossible; paradoxically, fidelity requires the judge to step outside the frame of instructions and exercise her own normative judgment. This theme is captured by what we have called reluctant judgment accounts of our constitutional practice.

One example of this turn of thought is Larry Lessig's work on constitutional translation.[2] Lessig argues that to be faithful to the instructions of the Constitution we have the conceptual burden of translating from one language to another, and then some. To paraphrase the waggish remark that the English and Americans are two peoples divided by a common language: We share with the framing generations a common language, but we are divided by profoundly different cultures. Translation involves sensitivity to both the context of writing and the context of application, and many elements in the two contexts may diverge, including (perhaps especially) firm presuppositions in the prevailing worldviews of these political generations so separated by time and circumstance. Translation inevitably involves a wide range of choice and judgment; it implicates a constitutional court in a practice that seems at times far removed from following instructions.

Another example of reluctant judgment theory is Bruce Ackerman's work centering on the claim that the Constitution can be and has been importantly amended by broad and sustained political consensus even though that consensus was not manifest in the way stipulated by Article V.[3] In certain times political concerns become superheated and politics are transformed from ordinary to constitutional; if an appropriate consensus forms in the crucible of constitutional politics, the distillate is an amendment to the Constitution, notwithstanding the absence of an Article V provenance. The job of a constitutional judge is to enforce the whole of the Constitution, including these informal amendments.

I find much to disagree with in this picture of constitutional amendment, a picture that I will address at length in Chapter 9. For the moment though, I want to focus on how Ackerman's provocative view gives license to judges to step outside their instructions and exercise their own normative judgment. The rough idea is this: While in principle judges are exclusively responsible to the Constitution's instructions, the Constitution includes important informal amendments like that which emerged from the New Deal. The effective Constitution is thus somewhat cluttered with overlapping and even contradictory instructions and judges are obliged to effectuate a synthesis among them. Thus, meaning has to be assigned to informal constitutional amendments, and then that meaning has to be reconciled with the Constitution as it was before. It is in the course of this reading of the unwritten and synthesis of the dense that the normative judgment of judges is engaged and overflows the role of simply following instructions.

What the models or metaphors of translation and synthesis have in common is a basal, unmitigated commitment to agency in principle, coupled with the discovery that pure or complete agency is impossible. For Lessig and Ackerman, the good judge aspires to take instructions, and is the best instruction-taker she can be. Were a stance of pure instruction-taking possible for the constitutional judge, she would maintain such a stance. But it is not possible: The instructions of the historical Constitution have to be translated or reconciled and the enterprise of translation or reconciliation inevitably engages independent normative judgment to some extent. It would be self-defeating to try to exclude these judgmental ingredients of adjudication, because we would ultimately have a product that was less rather than more faithful to the instructions of the past. The job description of a constitutional judge, for such theorists, thus begins with the instruction-taking imperative but is complicated by the necessary intrusion of normative independence. Judgment enters the story as an afterthought, as an inevitable but unfortunate limit on the instruction-taking mandate.

Reluctant judgment theories have an advantage over more recognizably originalist accounts of our constitutional practice. These, as we have seen, are transparently implausible. The broad generalities with which most of the liberty-bearing provisions of the Constitution are framed demand wide-bodied interpretation; they read as normative ideals, not as instructions for the resolution of specific cases or the fashioning of a systematic jurisprudence. The actual practice of constitutional adjudication, in turn, engages the ongoing normative judgment of the judiciary at every interesting point. Free speech, freedom of religion, and equality (equal protection)—all these important calls of the liberty-bearing Constitution demand and get the rich normative mediation of the judiciary for their implementation. Originalist judges and commentators themselves are routinely and rather notoriously embarrassed by the fact that they too have had to generate and defend accounts or theories of the abstract values named in the Constitution. Reluctant judgment theories can survive the force of these unduckable observations, because they agree—indeed, insist—that instruction-taking, unenlightened by appropriately pointed contemporary normative judgment, is an impossible judicial protocol.

But if reluctant judgment theories are more plausible than more extreme versions of the agency model of constitutional practice, their advantage is only a matter of degree, and ultimately, they are vulnerable to many of the same objections as those that greet their more extreme conceptual cousins. While reluctant judgment theories concede that conscientious constitutional instruction-takers must engage in independent normative judgment, they miss the point that the liberty-bearing provisions of the Constitution and our actual experience under them are starkly inconsistent with the idea that instruction-taking is the appropriate starting point for understanding our constitutional practice. The enterprise of bringing meaning to the Constitution involves at its core a collaboration between the framing generations who fixed the text of that document and those who undertake to apply the precepts named in the text to concrete issues that arise in the maintenance of our political community; both sides of that collaboration have to engage their faculties of normative judgment.

Were this not otherwise obvious, the Ninth Amendment would make it so. The Ninth Amendment puts the instruction-taking view of constitutional practice in conceptual gridlock. If the Constitution's text is understood to be the primary source of instruction for the judge, what is the conscientious instruction-taker supposed to do when the text itself tells her not to limit the scope of constitutional liberty to the rights stipulated in the Constitution? The instruction-taking judge: "I am bound to take my instructions from the Constitution; if the Constitution is silent, then I am bound to do nothing, that is, to leave the status quo absent my intervention in place." The Constitution: "I instruct you to intervene in some circumstances about which I am otherwise silent." The Ninth Amendment itself is open to interpretation, of course, but among its possible readings the most direct and plausible is exactly this. The hapless instruction-taking judge is thus in the position of the army barber who is ordered to shave every man on the post who does not shave himself.

We should not regard these features of the Constitution and/or our constitutional practice as causally accidental or normatively incidental. The generations responsible for framing the text of the Constitution could have chosen to speak in gritty detail rather than moral generality; in making the choice that they did, they depended upon the collaboration of those who would be responsible for implementing the broad values invoked in the Constitution's text. The Ninth Amendment, in turn, is best understood as responding to the worst fears of those who loved liberty but had doubts about the wisdom of including what ultimately became the Bill of Rights in the Constitution: that no simple list of the liberties of a free people could do justice to justice, and that, by the principle of *expressio unius est exclusio alterius,* a bill of rights would do more harm than good.

These choices of the framing generations are in turn causally connected to our constitutional structure. Article V was expected to make the Constitution obdurate to amendment and it succeeded in so doing to an extraordinary degree. Faced with the prospect of an extremely long-lived Constitution, and the requirements of Articles V and VII for a broad geographic consensus—a reasonable proxy for cultural consensus, especially at the most critical times in our constitutional history—the framing generations naturally opted for general moral commitments rather than a plethora of concrete instantiations of those commitments. Collaboration rather than instruction-taking is built into the structure of our constitutional practices, from the ground up.

This last observation brings us to a still more telling criticism of reluctant judgment theories. Because they maintain instruction-taking as the ideal, and make room for independent judgment only out of reluctant necessity, the reluctant judgment theorists are constrained to see our constitutional practices as they actually are as an embarrassment. The broad moral commands of the liberty-bearing provisions of the Constitution on their view must constitute a rather fundamental mistake, and the Ninth Amendment, unless it can be banished by construal, a disaster. Indeed, the very idea of a Constitution is rendered suspect if we regard popular judgment as talismanic and the independent judgment of the constitutional judiciary as unwelcome. An enduring constitution is almost certain to raise special problems of translation and synthesis as Lessig and Ackerman use those terms; parliamentary supremacy would surely reduce the independent judgmental freight of the judiciary. And even if in some preternatural way an enduring constitution could be crafted so as to issue complete instructions to judges and other public officials—instructions complete in the sense that they would not in principle require independent normative judgment on the part of the instruction-taker—why would we be inclined to let the judgment of political generations long since dead govern us today?

In contrast, the partnership model invites reflection on the practical virtues of our constitutional practices as they actually are. The partnership model is open to (indeed, depends upon) the belief that the collaboration between a popular constitutional decision-maker which paints in broad strokes and a judicial constitutional decision-maker which fills in these strokes with close and reflective detail is reasonably well suited to the enterprise of securing the fundamentals of political justice. This is the justice-seeking account of our constitutional practice, and I believe it to be the best account of that practice.

The reader may feel that I am forcing constitutional theory, and hence constitutional theorists, against an artificially sharp dichotomy between the agency model with its instruction-taking ideal and the partnership model with its collaborative ideal. It may appear that I have somehow lumbered reluctant judgment theory with conceptual entailments that it need not accept. But the point is this: Either we value the independent judgment of judges as collaborators in the constitutional project of identifying the fundamental demands of political justice or we do not. If we do not, then it makes perfectly good sense to regard the presence of such judgment in our constitutional practice as necessary but of no positive value—and more likely, of considerable negative value—outside the compass of that necessity. In turn, it makes perfectly good sense to cabin the license of judges to the bounds of that necessity. In contrast, if we do value the independent judgment of judges as an important part of a collaboration reasonably well suited to the important constitutional project of securing the fundamentals of political justice, then it is wrong to confine the exercise of that judgment to those circumstances where the exercise of judgment is parasitic to the task of following instructions. Constitutional theorists have to choose up, and I understand reluctant judgment theorists like Larry Lessig and Bruce Ackerman to have cast their lot with the impoverished agency model of our constitutional practice.

CHAPTER 5

Enter Partnership: The Justice-Seeking Account of Our Constitutional Practice

The Justice-Seeking Case

There are good reasons to see our constitutional practice in terms very different from the originalist, agency-centered account. The Constitution is not written like a tax code and has not been interpreted like one. Particularly in its liberty-bearing provisions, the Constitution offers broad structural propositions and moral generalities, and the judiciary has by and large accepted the obligation to fill in these general stipulations with concrete applications, to fashion workable and defensible conceptions of the Constitution's moral concepts. To be sure, this broad concession of responsibility to the judiciary requires explanation and justification. But without this understanding of the judicial role our constitutional practice would make very little sense. If the Constitution were only a piece of legislation elevated by its status to be primary over conflicting sources of law, we would have a hard time explaining why one generation's legislative impulses should govern persons living a century or two later; and why, further, we choose to interpose the effort and imperfection of historical reconstruction between a people and their laws. On the agency account, parliamentary democracy would seem to have considerable advantage over constitutionalism with its historical encumbrances.

To make sense of our constitutional practice, we have to see it as justice-seeking; that is, as serving the end of making our political community more just. Central to our constitutional practice is the partnership between the popular constitutional drafter who typically paints with broad strokes, and the judicial constitutional interpreter who is concerned with bringing rich content and close detail to the general principles announced in the text. The justice-seeking account of our constitutional practice depends upon the belief that this partnership, over time, will be a reasonably good guide to the most critical requirements of political justice.

It bears emphasis that this is a pragmatic judgment. The requirements of political justice are themselves matters of principle and often are best expressed or reflected upon in abstract terms; but the ability or tendency of real-world institutions to make decisions in conformity with those requirements is an exquisitely practical matter. In the end, confidence in this aspect of our constitutional practice may depend upon an assessment of our actual national experience in comparison with the experience of other nations. We have a sustained record of political, social, and religious liberty, and we have undone some of the worst features of our society by which the subordination of African-Americans and women has been perpetuated. With all its blemishes, this is an extraordinary national achievement, the value of which is underscored by the appeal of constitutionalism to many of the world's nations.[1] On the whole, a robust constitutional judiciary has been a substantial asset in securing these ends of a just society; the worst failings of the judiciary typically have been those of omission, instances in which a more active judicial role was demanded. There certainly are some blots on the record which count against active judicial review: The Dred Scott decision haunts anyone who looks honestly at our national experience, and most of us

regard the Lochner era as a sustained mistake of considerable propor-
tion. Still, when we learn of a foreign state abusing its citizens, many
of us find ourselves wishing that a courageous and independent
judiciary, with enough respect and authority to alter the course of
events, were in place. Our national experience justifies this moderated optimism in the judicial process.

THE STRUCTURAL VIRTUES OF THE JUDICIAL PROCESS

What can we say, then, of the structural features of constitutional
adjudication in support of the essential optimism of the justice-
seeking account of our constitutional practice? There are some familiar claims advanced on behalf of a robust constitutional judiciary
that may contain some truth, but are at best incomplete. One is
commonly offered in adagial form: "No one should be the judge of
his or her own cause." The job of measuring a popular political act
against constitutive principles of political justice ought not, this
claim goes, be left to the same entity that launched the act, since that
entity is not likely to be objective about its own conduct. But, even
without judicial review, a public body or official is seldom really the
sole arbiter of important political questions. Legislation originating
in one house of Congress or in one house of a state legislature—with
the exception of Nebraska, with its unicameral legislature—must
pass muster in the other house; and the President or the governor of
the state in question typically has the capacity to veto the legislation.
Moreover, the legislative process is likely to have begun only after at
least one committee has reviewed and approved the legislation. At
the local level, redundancy of a different sort is the norm. In the
land-use context, for example, a municipal legislative body, a chief
executive official, a zoning commission, a building department, and
a board of zoning appeals are likely to have substantial overlap in
responsibility and authority. In principle, at least, all of these popu-

lar political actors are subject to review by virtue of the electorate's choice of elected officials at reasonably frequent intervals.

Nor is it clear just whose "cause" a public deliberation is. Suppose the City Council of Indianapolis is considering legislation that imposes great liability on the producers and distributors of sexually explicit materials depicting women in certain ways. The City Council considers various arguments to the effect that women as a group are injured by the publication and distribution of these materials and deserve the protection offered by the legislation, and considers other arguments to the effect that the legislation would disserve badly the values protected by the First Amendment. In the end, the Council enacts the ordinance, and it quickly becomes the object of a constitutional challenge that works its way to the Supreme Court. The Supreme Court also hears arguments on both sides, addressed to the ordinance's constitutionality, but with much of the same content as the claims made before the City Council. The Court invalidates the ordinance on First Amendment grounds. At this point, both the Indianapolis City Council and the Supreme Court of the United States have performed public functions according (we are surely entitled to presume for these purposes) to their view of the public good. Both have made determinations as to the constitutionality of the law, with different results. To be sure, the Supreme Court's decision comes later, is focused more narrowly, and has final authority in our legal system. But it is hard to see in what useful sense the City Council is a judge in its own cause while the Supreme Court is not.

But lying just behind this claim is a deeper vision of the requirements of political justice and the distinct structure of adjudication in a constitutional court. At the heart of the social project of constitutional justice is the impartiality and generality of the moral perspective.[2] Common to much of our thinking about political morality in general, and about "rights" in particular, is the notion that the distinctive and essential character of the enterprise of political morality is its concern that the perspectives of each group, each class, and indeed each individual be taken seriously into account and somehow preserved, even in the clash of wills and interests that will inevitably characterize politics in a heterogeneous society such as our own. Political fairness emphatically is not understood as a simple matter of the force of will or welfare multiplied by the number of persons who advance either, but as a matter of fairness to each person, separately considered. Seen in the light of this moral ambition, the judiciary is particularly well structured to address questions of constitutional justice.

Judges are considerably more detached from the pressure of public opinion than are regularly elected public officials. Many judges are appointed for life, and most enjoy reasonably substantial job security; federal judges, with the guarantee of service for life at an undiminished salary are the model in this regard. The Constitution becomes important at exactly the point that public officials and the populace they serve take themselves to have good reasons to depart from constitutional norms, and the comparative independence of judges frees them from the potentially distorting influence of public will.

When a litigant appears before a judge, the litigant's claim is one of entitlement within a scheme of principle pursuant to which other persons have benefited in the past and other persons will benefit in the future. The subtle pervasiveness of principle in the hands of a judiciary committed to coherence requires that a judge at once understand the distinct claim of entitlement of the litigant before her and see the reach of that claim to other very different sorts of cases and litigants. There is a native drive to generality, to the abstraction of principle, to the very logic or grammar of rights.

For a judge, particular cases are just that—actual cases decided in the past by her own court or by courts to whose authority her own court is bound, and those she can imagine herself being called upon to decide in the future. The principles to which she is attracted as disposing rationales for the decision of the case before her must be considered against the backdrop of these past and future cases (future cases are of course hypothetical at the moment of decision), and, in the event of inconsistency, either the particular case outcomes or the more general and abstract rationales of decision must be remade (past outcomes are "remade" in the sense that a particular case or line of cases comes to be viewed as a mistake; future outcomes are "remade" in the sense that the judge reforms her ideas of how she should decide such a case were it to arise). Judges are responsible to both past decisions and future possibilities; they must test the principles upon which they are tempted to rely against these other outcomes, real and imagined. The enterprise of adjudication is thus a kind of institutional reflective equilibration. Judges are obliged to give each other and the broader audience of their opinions reasons for their decisions, and these reasons are of a special sort: They are in principle publicly accessible and publicly defensible, they are exemplars of what some philosophers have called "public reason." These features of constitutional adjudication are reinforced by the collegial, deliberative nature of constitutional tribunals in our legal system—most particularly, of the Supreme Court itself.

The constitutional judiciary has a specialized role with regard to political choices. Judges are steeped in the tradition of constitutional discourse, and their job is pointed towards the evaluation of governmental conduct against the norms of the Constitution. The judiciary is in the rough position of a quality control inspector examining some product for defects. Its job is specialized, and, in our constitutional tradition, largely negative. The judiciary has the responsibility of examining outcomes of the popular political process or other official behavior for inconsistency with constitutional precepts as understood appropriately. This is a special kind of redundancy. By introducing an interval of review keyed exclusively to those questions, it induces attention to questions of political justice and favors complaints of constitutional injustice, since if these complaints persuade at either the level of popular politics or the judiciary, they are fatal to what would be or actually is the outcome of other political impulses. We thus have an overall process of political decision-making which is called upon frequently to review itself self-consciously in terms of the fundamental principles of political justice which comprise our constitutional tradition.

Article V, Justice-Seeking, and Popular Constitutional Decision-Making

The justice-seeking account sees a transtemporal partnership at the heart of our constitutional practice. One partner consists of those persons in the founding or amending generations who participate in the utterance of the Constitution's text. The other partner consists of the judges who participate in the judicial interpretation of that text. Key is the idea of *partnership* as opposed to *agency:* Judges are not merely or even primarily instruction-takers; their independent normative judgment is expected and welcomed. The object of this partnership is the project of bringing our political community better into conformity with fundamental requirements of political justice.

The partnership at the center of our justice-seeking constitutional practice has a characteristic structure: At least with regard to the liberty bearing provisions of the Constitution, the popular constitutional decision-maker typically speaks at a high level of generality and of moral abstraction. The job of the constitutional judiciary thus becomes applying very general constitutional commitments to concrete cases, with the concomitant obligations of generating case-spanning doctrine and moral understandings which choose among competing accounts of the Constitution's lofty norms.

This devolution of responsibility is itself a product of our constitutional structure. Article V of the Constitution requires the support of a supermajority of the states for any amendment, much as Article VII required such a supermajority for the launching of the Constitution initially. It was anticipated that the Constitution would be hard to amend, and in practice it has been remarkably so. Far from regarding this obduracy to change as an embarrassment, the justice-seeking account sees it as a virtue: By forcing would-be popular constitutional decision-makers to secure broad inter-state and inter-regional consensus, and by making them aware that they are drafting not just for themselves but for their children and their children's children, Article V inspires constitutional choices of the right kind. It inspires, that is, the choice of widely acceptable, general, and abstract precepts, precepts which in turn facilitate the working partnership with the constitutional judiciary.

Obviously, on this view judges are not merely taking instructions in some mechanical sense; neither, it should be emphasized, are they merely "translating" instructions from a culturally different past or synthesizing overlapping and conflicting instructions from different constitutional epochs. These more subtle understandings of constitutional judges as instruction-takers still regard the basal obligation of the constitutional judge as that of being the best instruction-taker she can be, and make room for the independent normative judgment of constitutional judges and courts only grudgingly, as the paradoxical and unfortunate consequence of the instruction-taking venture. Justice-seeking constitutionalism, in contrast, welcomes the independent judgmental role of judges as well-suited to the enterprise that is its namesake.

The Conceptual Burdens of
the Justice-Seeking Account

If we are otherwise attracted to the justice-seeking account of our constitutional practice, we have to address several problems which it presents. These problems will be the focus of the remainder of this book. In the end, I hope not only to have addressed them to the satisfaction of my readers, and hence made the case for the justice-seeking account: I hope as well to have demonstrated that one of the virtues of this account is that it both invites and suggests answers to these questions, and thus inspires a more complete understanding of our constitutional practice.

THE DURABLE MORAL SHORTFALL OF
CONSTITUTIONAL DOCTRINE

Constitutional case law is thin in this important sense: The range of those matters that are plausible candidates for judicial engagement and enforcement in the name of the Constitution is considerably smaller than the range of those matters that are plausibly understood to implicate serious questions of political justice. This moral short-fall is one of the most durable and salient features of our constitutional life, one that begs for explanation.

Plausible accounts of political justice and stable understandings of constitutional case law seem particularly discrepant in two areas. The first is economic justice: In the post-Lochner era constitutional courts have been systematically unconcerned with economic inequities. The Takings Clause is the only place where economic rights survive at all, and even as the Takings Clause begins to acquire some vigor[3] it remains a quite narrow limitation on the rather extreme imposition of only one form of economic hardship.

The scope of the domain thus put beyond the reach of constitutional case law is considerable. Our constitutional jurisprudence singles out comparatively few encounters between the state and its citizens as matters of serious judicial concern. After threats to speech, religion, and the narrow band of activities that fall under the rubric of privacy, after the disfavor of persons because of their race or gender (or possibly, because of their sexual orientation, their nationality, or the marital status of their parents), and after lapses from fairness in criminal process, the attention of the constitutional judiciary rapidly falls off.[4] By default, everything else falls in the miasma of economic rights. Thus, the claim of a person to grow and dispense herbs as a calling would be doomed to the losing invocation of equal protection or due process, and the only claim of a person displaced from her home by governmental activity is compensation for its value.

The most vivid discrepancy between constitutional case law and political justice concerns a particular aspect of our economic life— the welfare of the poor. Justice ought to insist that our institutions be arranged so that persons who are willing to make reasonable efforts on their own behalf enjoy the ability to secure the minimum necessities of a decent life; but constitutional claims pointing towards minimum welfare rights have been systematically rebuffed. It is hard to imagine an attractive view of political justice that would be as blind to hunger, poverty, and radical skews in wealth and opportunity as has been the judiciary's reading of the Constitution at any moment in our history.[5]

The second area of marked discrepancy between constitutional case law and political justice is the repair of the harms of historic injustice. When the Federal Communications Commission adopts a preference for minority-owned radio stations, or when Congress forbids racial discrimination by private employers, we can readily understand these acts as improving the state of justice, as redressing the entrenched consequences of institutional racism that was once supported by law. If we believe, as we must, that slavery and its aftermath of legally endorsed racial caste was deeply unjust; and if we believe, as we should, that we continue to suffer social and economic divisions along the fault lines of race as a consequence of our history, it follows that justice not merely permits but requires the repair of this injustice. But nothing in constitutional case law anticipates the judicial enforcement of this obligation.

The observation that a broad gap exists between our notions of political justice and the corpus of constitutional case law could be read as simply offering a good reason to reconsider and expand constitutional doctrine. Certainly there is something to this. We should be careful not to let our sometimes timid exploration of the boundaries of constitutional justice limit our reflective imagination. But the disparity between political justice and constitutional case law seems deeper, more durable, and more natural than can be accounted for by claims that constitutional doctrine should be more robust. Few would be tempted by the view that the judiciary ought to enforce perfect economic justice in the name of the Constitution, whatever the precincts of such justice are taken to be. And it does not seem jarring that racial preferences and prohibitions of private racial discrimination be understood as constitutional—indeed, as clearly constitutionally desirable—yet not be treated by the judiciary as required by the Constitution. We neither expect nor desire the constitutional judiciary to congest political choice to the full extent of justice.

Were we drawn to the originalist account of our constitutional practice, the idea that the Constitution might fall short of the aspirations of justice would be unproblematic. For whatever reason—failed judgment, truncated ambition, the limits of foresight, narrowed political consensus, or an urge to constitutionalize piecemeal—the constitutional "legislature" would be understood simply to have stopped legislating at various arbitrary points. Constitutional judges, in turn, would be understood as limited to the boundary inscribed by these points, as bound by a positivist tether to the incomplete or partial constitutional project. What would be remarkable, on this account, would be the conclusion that the Constitution and political justice were to any substantial degree congruent.

But the originalist account is a failed representation of our constitutional practice; and if we take up the justice-seeking account in its stead, the idea of the Constitution stopping measurably short of the aspirations of justice becomes very problematic indeed. Now, we have to explain how our constitutional practice has justice as its ambition, but systematically holds back from extending its reach appropriately far.

This is a critical question about our constitutional practice, one which takes us deep into the architecture of that practice. To capture that surprisingly complex architecture, I will make two passes: In Chapters 6 and 7, I will defend and explore the implications of the proposition that the Constitution is and should be judicially *under-enforced*—that there is a gap between the judicially enforced Constitution and the full normative reach of constitutional justice. In Chapter 8, I will identify and explore the implications of a second gap—a gap between the domain of *constitutional* justice and justice at its broadest reaches. Together, these gaps explain the legitimate dimension of the moral shortfall of the adjudicated Constitution.

THE PROBLEMATIC STATUS OF ARTICLE V

A second question provoked by the justice-seeking account concerns the problematic status of the Constitution's stipulated rules for amendment. In the justice-seeking account, the open texture of the Constitution's liberty-bearing provisions is neither incidental nor accidental. The demand these provisions make on the engaged normative judgment of the constitutional judiciary is not an embarrassment, but a virtue of our constitutional affairs; and it is not an accident, but rather a product of responsible constitutional choice in the face of a Constitution rightfully expected to be obdurate to change. But that obduracy is in part a function of the requirements that Article V places on amendment, and Article V has been called into doubt on two related grounds. First, several commentators have seriously questioned whether Article V is the exclusive means of amending the Constitution, or whether there are other routes to amendment, including some routes in which the Constitution could be unconsciously or unwittingly amended in a period of sustained political activity on the part of a mobilized national constituency. Indeed, these commentators could be read as questioning whether any Constitution can bind a democratic people to a mechanism for constitutive change. Second, this Article V skepticism makes best sense when viewed against a more widely held view, namely, that Article V obduracy to review is inconsistent with democratic principles.

In Chapter 9, we will take up what could be called the birth logic of a democratic constitution, and explore in some detail the reasons a democratic people have for choosing a demanding representation of "the people" for purposes of constitutional choice, thereby making their constitution obdurate to change. We will also consider the puzzling relationship between a democratic people and their chosen self-representation, pursuant to which it is entirely appropriate to regard stipulated rules for constitutional change as exclusive and binding.

But this leaves open the question of whether the degree and form of obduracy brought to our Constitution by Article V is consistent with democracy. That more particularized question will be taken up in Chapter 10, along with other democratic concerns.

DEMOCRACY

The justice-seeking account of our constitutional practice encounters and responds to concerns about democracy at almost every turn. The idea that the Constitution is and should be judicially underenforced depends on institutional differences that favor popular political processes, in important part on democratic grounds. So too, the idea that the whole of constitutional justice is confined to a domain that is more narrow than the full range of political justice depends in important part on the fact that some claims of constitutional justice come wrapped in questions of strategy and responsibility that necessarily belong to popular political judgment. There is yet another claim sounding in democracy that we will take up and ultimately reject. This is the claim common and crucial to what we have described above as "democratarian" theories, namely, that the exclusive province of justice-seeking constitutionalism should be the perfecting of the process of democratic choice.

In Chapter 10, our last chapter, we will return to Article V. In the end, democratic objections to Article V will prove to be closely connected to democratic objections to the very idea of judicially enforced constitutionalism; and the justice-seeking account will play an important positive role in understanding the mistake upon which those deeper objections rest. Key to this discussion is the recognition that the deliberative features of constitutional adjudication offer a distinct and distinctly democratic form of equal participation in the process of rights contestation. That realization, in turn, will both inform our consideration of Article V and offer grounds for resisting the idea that constitutional judges should shade their judgments to avert political controversy.

So that is the balance of our agenda: Underenforcement; the Domain of Constitutional Justice; the Birth Logic of a Democratic Constitution; and Democracy and the Justice-Seeking Constitution.

CHAPTER 6

The Thinness of Constitutional Law and the Underenforcement Thesis

The Moral Shortfall of Constitutional Law

Justice-seeking theorists have the burden of explaining why the Constitution is so thin, why it stops so far short of justice if justice is its target. Constitutional law plainly does not address all of political justice. Consider, for example, these two claims: that members of our political community are entitled to economic arrangements that offer them minimally decent material lives in exchange for hard work on their own behalf; and that government is obliged to make reasonable efforts to undo structurally entrenched social bias against vulnerable racial groups and women. Neither of these principles has now or has ever had any apparent life in constitutional doctrine.[1] This is not hard to explain on the originalist account: Constitutional law runs out because the moral imagination or generosity of the founding and amending generations ran out, and there is nothing more to explain. But if we understand the Constitution to be justice-seeking, then we have to explain how judicial implementations of it have failed to seriously approach—much less secure—what many of us at least would regard as important and unduckable requirements of political justice.

The justice-seeking account acknowledges the guidance of constitutional text, history, and established doctrine, of course, and it might be in these conventional legal constraints that a partial explanation for the moral shortfall of constitutional law is to be found. But the sharp refusal of constitutional law to embrace claims like the right to minimum welfare and the obligation to reform entrenched bias is too durable, too widely endorsed, and insufficiently founded on the dictates of text and history to be accounted for on these grounds alone.

Consider the Constitution's pointed indifference to poverty. On any plausible account, law is inertial. The broad structure and narrow detail of past political events exert a direct and significant effect on present choices: Enacted text and prior adjudication bind imperfectly and incompletely, but bind they certainly do. As a result, there will almost always be some discrepancy between the best choice available to a legal decision-maker, as evaluated in isolation from the historical claims of law, and the best legal decision. Constitutional law too, of course, is to some meaningful degree tied to past political events. There is the text and structure of the Constitution to be reckoned with as well as the historical stream of decisions by the Supreme Court and the federal and state judiciaries the Court superintends. There are also broad patterns of congressional and presidential behavior over time, reflecting implicit and occasionally explicit and self-conscious judgments of constitutional rectitude. Accordingly, some disparity between justice and constitutional case law is the inevitable product of constitutional law's responsibility to our constitutional past; all law is in this way and to this degree at odds with ideal justice. Indeed, in this sense, the failure of constitutional law to perfectly capture justice is necessary to its soundness.

The native, inertial imperfection of law, however, cannot fully account for constitutional case law's limited grasp. The liberty-bearing provisions of the Constitution speak at a broad conceptual pitch, and over time, constitutional case law has shown itself to be remarkably pliable in the service of the rectification of perceived injustice. But economic justice for the suffering poor has never secured a firm place on the Court's constitutional agenda. Even the Warren Court in its most aggressive moments approached the question of economic justice with oblique caution. Throughout, the feeling has not been one of reluctant fidelity but rather of active judgment that recognizes sharp limitations on the reach of constitutional principle or, in the alternative, on the reach of judicially accessible constitutional principle. The sense that seems pervasive in modern constitutional adjudication and most commentary is that judicial enforcement of economic justice would inappropriately congest popular political choice. Something more than mere inertia is needed to explain how a justice-seeking Constitution could treat as a virtue the durable, systematic refusal to respond to the claims of the suffering poor.

Distinguishing between the Constitution and Its Judicial Enforcement

An important part of the moral shortfall of our constitutional law can be explained by the gap between the Constitution proper and the adjudicated Constitution. We have a tendency to equate the two, treating the scope of a constitutional norm as coterminous with the scope of its judicial enforcement. Thus, when the Supreme Court declines to inquire seriously into an arguably unjust distinction drawn between classes of persons or enterprises in a state tax or regulatory statute, this decision is nominally expressed and widely understood as an authoritative determination that the distinction does not violate the Equal Protection Clause.

But where a federal judicial construct is found not to extend to certain official behavior because of institutional concerns rather than analytical perceptions, it seems strange to regard the resulting decision as a statement about the meaning of the constitutional norm in question. After all, what the members of the federal tribunal have actually determined in such a case is that there are good reasons for stopping short of exhausting the content of the constitutional concept with which they are dealing; the limited judicial construct which they have fashioned or accepted is occasioned by this determination and does not derive from a judgment about the scope of the constitutional concept itself.

Some principles of political justice are wrapped in complex choices of strategy and responsibility that are properly the responsibility of popular political institutions. When confronting constitutional principles that are entangled in this way, the judiciary justifiably declines to enforce the Constitution to its outermost margins, and defers—at least in the first instance—to the political branches of the state and federal governments. The right to minimum welfare and the obligation to reform structurally entrenched social bias are two good examples of precepts of political justice that are for this reason justifiably underenforced by the judiciary.

Consider just one component of the right to minimum welfare: minimally adequate medical care. Recent national experience stands as a reminder of the questions that implementation of such a right will entail: What level of medical care is minimally adequate? How should such care be provided—by general financial support, single payer or managed competition insurance, medical vouchers or clinics for the poor? What level or levels of government should be responsible for design, oversight, and support of the program? How should the financial burden of such a program be distributed, and how should the distribution of this burden be implemented? All of these decisions of strategy and responsibility remain on the table even after we have accepted the basic norm of a right to minimum welfare and identified medical care as one of its critical components.

These are powerful reasons why the judicial enforcement of the Constitution stops short of affirmative ingredients of justice like the right to minimum welfare and the obligation of government to reform entrenched racial and gender bias. They are not good reasons for supposing that the Constitution itself—as opposed to the adjudicated Constitution—similarly falls short of addressing these fundamental elements of political justice.

Constitutional norms should be understood to be legally valid to their full conceptual limits, and federal judicial decisions which stop short of these limits should be understood as delineating only the boundaries of the federal courts' role in enforcing the norm. By "legally valid," I mean that the unenforced margins of underenforced norms should have the full status of positive law which we generally accord to the norms of our Constitution, save only that the federal judiciary will not enforce these margins. Thus, the legal powers or legal obligations of government officials which are subtended in the unenforced margins of underenforced constitutional norms are to be understood to remain in full force.

For some this view may be troubling because of our tendency, reinforced by the practical dominance of the Supreme Court as the final arbiter of our constitutional affairs, to equate the existence of a constitutional norm with the possibility of its enforcement against an offending official. But the notion that to be legally obligated means to be vulnerable to external enforcement can have only a superficial appeal. Consider the case of the judges of the highest court of a state when they rule on a matter of state law, or of the justices of the Supreme Court of the United States when they address matters within the federal sphere. We are quite comfortable in the belief that these judges are legally obligated to observe the norms of their legal system. It could be argued that there exist exceptional mechanisms like impeachment to enforce compliance with the judicial duty to operate within the norms specifying their own powers and duties and to apply faithfully the appropriate rules of decision to cases before them. Yet surely the presence of such rarely invoked enforcement devices is not essential to our perception that these judges are routinely and consistently bound to legal standards. To suggest that a judge's duty was limited to whatever view she chose to take of her own powers and of the legal norms she was called on to apply would conform neither to the general conception of a judge's responsibility nor to the understanding that judges themselves share of their legal responsibility.

The idea that the judicially enforced scope of a constitutional norm may be narrower than its scope as legal authority enjoys a venerable provenance. James Bradley Thayer's essay on "The Origin and Scope of the American Doctrine of Constitutional Law" is an important intellectual fount of the judicial restraint thesis. Thayer argued for the rule of clear mistake—that "an Act of the legislature ... [ought] not to be declared void unless the violation of the constitution is so manifest as to leave no room for reasonable doubt."[2] Thayer's rule of clear mistake was not founded on the idea that only manifestly abusive legislative enactments are unconstitutional, but rather on the idea that only such manifest error entitles a court to displace the prior constitutional ruling of the enacting legislature. It was offered as a rule of judicial behavior—or, in Thayer's words, a "rule of administration." Thayer underscores this proposition with the following paraphrase of Thomas M. Cooley: "[O]ne who is a member of a legislature may vote against a measure as being, in his judgment, unconstitutional; and, being subsequently placed on the bench, when this measure, having been passed by the legislature in spite of his opposition, comes before him judicially, may there find it his duty, although he has in no degree changed his opinion, to declare it constitutional."[3]

Thayer's unrefined and uninflected demand for judicial restraint has not prevailed, of course. In a number of contexts where the guarantees of the Constitution implicate fundamental values of political justice, the modern Supreme Court has assumed a primary and vigorous role of enforcement, a role which is from start to finish inconsistent with Thayerian deference to legislative judgment. In the face of this positive and visible feature of constitutional adjudication, we have a tendency to ignore an important, albeit negative and invisible feature: Outside the comparatively narrow areas where the Court has adopted a stance of active constitutional oversight, a tradition of judicial restraint reigns; and in this broad residual area of judicial passivity, judicial decisions to approve the conduct of various government actors may well represent the Court's judgment of its institutional role rather than exhaustive analyses of the meaning of the implicated constitutional norms.

In one context, we do clearly distinguish between a determination that there exist decisive reasons for the judiciary to decline to apply a norm of the Constitution to a given set of facts and a determination that the norm in question does not reach that set of facts. This distinction, in fact, is the conceptual basis of the political question doctrine. Suppose that a proceeding is brought against the Secretary of the Department of Agriculture, seeking to enjoin her from further engaging in certain conduct that is asserted to be unconstitutional. Imagine now two possible judicial holdings: (1) the Secretary's conduct does not violate the specified norms of the Constitution; (2) it is inappropriate for this court to inquire whether the Secretary's conduct violates the specified norms of the Constitution. The first holding would be a constitutional judgment on the merits; the second, an invocation of the political question doctrine. The second is sensibly distinguished from the first only if we continue to think of the constitutional norms in question as being legally valid, and understand the court to have determined only that it cannot enforce them. The very existence of the political question doctrine in our constitutional jurisprudence thus reflects a partial recognition of the idea of judicial underenforcement.

This view of the meaning of a judicial invocation of the political question doctrine is reinforced by official behavior under circumstances in which the doctrine insulates that behavior from judicial accountability. Two prominent examples of such circumstances are provided by the executive prosecution of the Vietnam War and the impeachment proceedings against Richard Nixon and William Clinton.

As to the prosecution of hostilities in Indochina, the federal judiciary from the first indicated that it would not intervene. And while there was some scholarly support for judicial intervention in the impeachment process, such intervention was in fact extremely unlikely. Nevertheless, in both contexts, official protagonists devoted a great deal of energy to arguments about the constitutionality of official behavior. If anything, the improbability or impossibility of judicial intervention encouraged the relevant governmental actors to take—or at least appear to take—special pains to measure their conduct against the norms of the Constitution.

* * *

We began this inquiry by noting that the justice-seeking account of constitutionalism calls attention to a noteworthy feature of our constitutional practice: Constitutional law, at the hands of the judiciary, falls systematically short of addressing what many would regard as obvious requirements of a just political community. There is, as we have seen, good reason for the judiciary to stop short of enforcing such requirements in the name of the Constitution, but these are reasons that speak to the institutional limitations of the judiciary, not to the best understanding of the Constitution itself. A view of our constitutional practice that acknowledges the existence of a legitimate and potentially substantial gap between the scope of judicial enforcement of the Constitution and the scope of the Constitution itself can better serve these distinct conceptual masters than one which insists on linking them. Hence the underenforcement thesis.

CHAPTER 7

The Conceptual Salience
of Underenforcement

Though startling on first encounter, perhaps, the underenforcement thesis is becoming more and more of a commonplace in constitutional discourse. Within the community of constitutional scholars, underenforcement is widely accepted, and forms an integral part of a good deal of contemporary constitutional analysis. And recently, within the constitutional judiciary itself, the idea of underenforcement has begun to enjoy a place on the conceptual agenda.

But why does it matter whether we regard the discrepancy between the reach of constitutional case law and the reach of political justice as explainable—at least in important part—in terms of the limits of constitutional adjudication, or whether we simply see the Constitution itself as stopping considerably short of the full measure of political justice? The most natural place to look for the significance of these competing explanations for the thinness of constitutional case law would lie in their implications for legislators. Both underenforcement and the more blunt alternative, after all, seek to explain constitutional case law more or less as we find it, thinness and all. The promise of underenforcement would seem most naturally to lie in the obligations it imposes on political actors outside the courts, obligations which, by hypothesis, will elude judicial enforcement. Underenforcement recognizes that the Constitution is broader than judicially articulated constitutional law, and that non-judicial political actors have a corresponding obligation to interpret and respect the Constitution to its outermost margins.

If this is the only direction in which we look to establish the salience of the underenforcement thesis, however, we will encounter reasons for some doubt. Suppose a legislator must choose between two legislative options, anticipates that the judiciary would uphold each option as constitutionally valid, but believes that the appropriate reading of the Constitution (as opposed to the judiciary's likely reading) condemns one option. Surely, she will see herself as bound to avoid the unconstitutional option. But what if the legislator believes, in contrast, that while both options are constitutional, one option is unjust? Without more, we can assume that she again will see herself as bound, this time to avoid the unjust course of action. Further, in the hypothesized absence of the prospect of judicial enforcement of either obligation, it is not clear that the two forms of her obligation differ in kind or intensity. We cannot imagine, for example, that she could sensibly say aloud or to herself, "I've taken an oath to support and defend the Constitution, but avoiding injustice is not part of my job description."

But other important consequences do flow from the underenforcement thesis. What follows is a partial canvass of these consequences, an exercise with several ambitions. First, I hope to show that the underenforcement thesis—upon which the justice-seeking account importantly depends—fits extant practice better than the more conventional, what-you-see-is-all-there-is view of constitutional substance. Second, I hope to shore up aspects of extant constitutional doctrine that are conceptually problematic absent the clarifying support of the underenforcement thesis. Third, and perhaps most importantly, I hope to suggest directions that the Court ought to take but has not to date taken in response to the insights offered by the underenforcement thesis.

Underenforcement and the Right to Minimum Welfare

We can begin by returning one more time to the question of a right to minimum welfare. In some cases, the Court ought to be able to act on entitlements associated with minimum welfare, once other institutions of government have acted and created contexts in which the issue of right surfaces largely unencumbered by other questions. Thus, underenforcement offers a better understanding of *Plyler v. Doe*,[1] where the Court held that the exclusion of illegal immigrants from the Texas public schools was unconstitutional. Equal protection jurisprudence did not offer the Plyler Court a means of expressing its strong sense of injustice. The Court was not prepared to treat the minor children of illegal immigrants as a suspect class, nor to treat education as a fundamental right. The first would have claimed too much on behalf of the children whose parents were distinguished precisely by the illegality of their immigration status, and the second would have established exactly the sort of affirmative entitlement systematically avoided in constitutional doctrine. But Justice Brennan, who wrote for the majority, and Justices Marshall, Blackmun, and Powell, who authored separate concurring opinions, all focused on essentially the same thing: the great importance of education for the life prospects of the young, impoverished victims of Texas's exclusionary policy.[2]

Missing from the Court's conceptual vocabulary was a means of capturing what the justices in the majority knew: (1) that it is unjust for a state to arrange its institutions so that any child is denied an adequate education; (2) that the constitutional judiciary cannot appropriately decide what an adequate education is or how it ought to be provided; and (3) that once Texas had created a system of public education, the unjust exclusion from that system of children who could receive no other education was judicially remediable. If we acknowledge that there is a discrepancy between the scope of constitutional justice and the scope of constitutional case law, and that the right to an adequate education falls squarely in the gap, we have the appropriate vocabulary at hand. The Texas children had a constitutional right to an adequate education, but the responsibility for recognizing that right in the first instance fell on local, state, and federal legislators. However, once a system of free public education was in place, it was within the competence of the constitutional judiciary to insist that every child have access.

Plyler may be seen as evidence that the Court could not live without an analytical structure that it had already decided it could not live with—namely, the "fundamental rights" strand of equal protection doctrine. Now widely regarded as a failed Warren Court experiment, the idea behind this aspect of equal protection jurisprudence was that selective distribution of certain important interests was constitutionally dubious and should accordingly be subject to the rigors of the compelling state interest test.

Applied to laws that gave some persons the right to vote and denied that right to others, this approach was unproblematic—a roundabout way of recognizing that there is a constitutionally protected right of competent persons within a jurisdiction to participate equally in elections. But applied to welfare benefits, the fundamental rights approach seemed to make no sense. If persons are constitutionally entitled to receive benefit X, the argument ran, then nothing is added to their claim by the observation that others are already getting X. Conversely, if persons are not entitled to receive benefit X, then—barring an illicit criterion of selection—the fact that some are receiving X is not enough to create an entitlement in those who are not. Equal protection is being asked to do the work of substantive entitlement, and along the way an interest is being en-larged to the status of a right.

The impulse behind the Warren Court's fundamental rights ju-risprudence can be seen in a more favorable light, however, if we recognize that the judiciary does not enforce the entire Constitution and if we further recognize rights to minimum welfare as an instance of underenforcement. Then an ongoing benefits program—com-plete with funding, administration, and ballpark criteria of need—invites a bifurcation of role: The legislature has already resolved the questions of social strategy and responsibility from which the Court has shied, and what remains for adjudication is the claim of consti-tutional right shorn of its massive entailments of social strategy and responsibility.

This understanding of *Plyler* does not argue for close judicial scrutiny of every distinction in eligibility and level of entitlement in welfare programs; that approach would land the judiciary in the middle of the same issues of strategy and responsibility that under-enforcement avoids in the first place. But this understanding does encourage close attention to, and skepticism of, categorical exclu-sions of the needy from benefits that would ameliorate their need, especially when those exclusions seem related not to fairness among the needy or to strategies of care, but rather to selective failures of concern.

Plyler is not unique in reflecting both the instinct and capacity of the judiciary to intervene in order to protect the right to mini-mum welfare against unjust categorical exclusions. One group of exclusions from the elements of minimum welfare is naturally sus-picious: When a state has in place programs that serve the aim of providing a welfare safety net, but then bars its newest citizens from the full protection of these programs, it is natural to suspect that an uncaring sense of us-versus-them—an unsavory form of federal nativism—has triumphed over judgments of need or desert. The Supreme Court has for more than half a century waged war on this sort of unjust denial of the elements of minimum welfare.

In earlier cases such as *Shapiro v. Thompson*[3] and *Memorial Hospital v. Maricopa County*,[4] the Court struck down durational residency requirements that barred new arrivals from the enjoyment of public benefits critical to their basic welfare. Its rationale for so doing was the "right to travel," the driving idea being that residency requirements of this sort impose a severe penalty on persons who exercise their right to migrate from one state to another. But, in other contexts, the Court was far less wary of durational residency requirements, and the Court's sensitivity to the right to travel in these cases makes a good deal more sense if we link it to the basic welfare concerns at stake.[5]

More recently, the Court considered the constitutionality of a California rule limiting newly arrived indigent families for the first twelve months of their residency to the level of basic welfare payments to which they would have been entitled in the state from which they emigrated. Now the penalty rationale of the earlier right to travel cases seemed inapt, since these families were not necessarily worse off by virtue of their having exercised their right to move from one state to another. The Court responded in *Saenz v. Roe*[6] by striking down this form of durational residency requirement as well. Not only does the Constitution bar legislation that penalizes persons for moving between states, the Court concluded, it also makes suspect any adverse treatment of newly arrived residents. The basis of this new antidiscrimination principle for the *Saenz* Court was the Privileges or Immunities Clause of the Fourteenth Amendment, which provides that "No state shall make or enforce any law which shall abridge the privileges or immunities of Citizens of the United States." This was big news indeed, since the clause in question, though begging in its terms for a serious role in our constitutional life, has never had one, and seems by its terms far better suited to the invocation of fundamental rights against the conduct of the states than to the support of a principle barring intrastate distinctions between new state residents and their more settled counterparts. Nor is the principle itself irresistible: Many states require that students age-in as residents for substantial periods before they come to enjoy the benefits of reduced tuition at state universities, and the justness of such requirements would seem to some at least to run deeper than the practical need to establish the bona fides of state residency. Like the earlier right to travel cases, *Saenz* makes much more sense if understood as the invalidation of an unjust categorical exclusion from the benefits of a state-established safety net—if understood, in other words, as an instance of the secondary judicial protection of the constitutional right to minimum welfare. So understood, these cases of judicial enforcement of the right to minimum welfare are secondary in this sense: The judiciary steps in only after the programmatic choices of strategy and responsibility have been made, and polices the resulting programs against the possibility of unjust, categorical exclusions.

There are several other cases that fit this description, each of which would be anomalous in our constitutional tradition were they not so understood. Consider *United States Department of Agriculture v. Moreno*[7] and *United States Department of Agriculture v. Murry*.[8] In these cases, the Court struck down a congressional attempt to disqualify persons living in communal arrangements from the food stamp program. The Court could find no traditional doctrinal hook for its rulings, but made the opaque pronouncement that congressional antipathy to persons living in communal arrangements was simply not the kind of interest that could support a governmental classification. These cases have never been well understood, and have given rise to very little useful doctrine. But if we remember that food for the hungry is at stake, and see *Moreno* and *Murry* as part of the Court's secondary enforcement role, they make much more sense. The same can be said of *City of Cleburne v. Cleburne Living Center*,[9] where the Court struck down a municipal ordinance that barred group homes for handicapped persons. The Court was at pains in *Cleburne* to decline to make handicapped persons a suspect class; and any thought that *Cleburne* was a way station on the road to a later finding of suspect class status was dashed by the Court's more recent decision in *Alabama v. Garrett*,[10] which we will discuss later in this chapter. *Cleburne* is inconsistent with equal protection doctrine then or now, and a genuinely puzzling albeit sympathetic decision—unless we focus on what makes it such a sympathetic decision, and join Justices Marshall, Blackmun, and Brennan in the understanding that group living is the only feasible way that the mentally retarded can lead minimally decent lives.[11]

It bears emphasis that *Moreno, Murry,* and *Cleburne* are not judicial sports, momentary lapses of sound judicial judgment. On the contrary, each continues to be cited with approval and with some regularity at that. And they are cases with considerable intuitive appeal. But they beg for conceptual reconciliation with the rest of our constitutional tradition, and underenforcement offers precisely that.

This is not to suggest that the line between permissible and impermissible judicial interventions is an easy one to draw, or that cases like *Plyler* will inevitably display clear outcomes when viewed through the lens of underenforcement and the constitutional right to minimum welfare. But important chunks of the Court's jurisprudence make much more sense in these terms, and future cases will be better understood and responded to if the division of constitutional labor implicated by underenforcement is recognized and acted upon.

Goldberg v. Kelly[12] and its progeny offer a procedural variation on this theme. An early outpost of the "new property," *Goldberg* gave the recipients of basic welfare grants a due process right to an evidentiary hearing prior to the termination of their benefits. *Goldberg* ushered in the modern era in which the beneficiaries of governmental resources enjoy at least some due process rights, if they have a "property" interest in continuing to receive those resources. However, *Goldberg* is unique in the line it spawned: No other case has required a pretermination evidentiary hearing. In *Mathews v. Eldridge*,[13] the Court distinguished *Goldberg* in this respect, emphasizing that welfare benefits go to persons on "the very margin of subsistence."[14] Also protected after *Goldberg* are due process rights where "liberty" interests are at stake. But almost from the outset, the Court has been wary of finding liberty interests in the civil context.[15] In the midst of a general picture of subdued fidelity to due process rights, *Goss v. Lopez*[16] stands out. Finding both liberty and property interests to be at stake, the Court in *Goss* held that elementary and secondary students in public schools had the right to hearings, not only prior to expulsion, but prior to suspensions, even short-term suspensions.

Goldberg launched the due process revolution and *Goss* was impervious to the tacit counterrevolution that deprived *Goldberg* of much of its force. Once underenforcement is introduced into the picture, this can be explained as something other than a coincidence, a freak of stare decisis, or a product of soft hearts leading to soft heads. The underenforcement thesis can explain—and should secure—outcomes like these. (I do not mean to live or die with the proposition that very short-term suspensions from public school qualify for predeprivation hearings, but rather with the view that important procedural rights attach to attendance at public school generally.) Basic welfare payments and public education at the elementary and secondary levels ought to be understood as constitutional entitlements, the primary provision of which is the constitutional responsibility of nonjudicial governmental bodies. Once the broad structural features of programs providing the entitlements are in place, the judiciary can respond constructively in a number of ways. Assuring that appropriate process protects the beneficiaries of these entitlements is a compelling feature of the judiciary's secondary role with regard to such entitlements.

Underenforcement and Congressional Authority

At the heart of the underenforcement thesis is the idea of a constitutional division of labor. If the judiciary is constrained by durable features of its institutional role from fully enforcing the Constitution, it follows that we should encourage and welcome the assistance of other governmental actors in realizing more fully the Constitution's aims. This general premise of divided constitutional labor is especially important with regard to Congress's authority to enforce the Reconstruction Amendments.

In the aftermath of the Civil War, the architecture of governmental authority to enforce the fundamental requirements of political justice was restructured in basic and enduring ways. The Thirteenth, Fourteenth, and Fifteenth Amendments to the Constitution—the so-called Reconstruction Amendments—are the textual predicates of this restructuring. Together, they (1) abolish slavery; (2) insist on the rights of equal citizenship for all members of our political community, including and especially those disfavored by reason of race; and (3) make the justness of state and local governmental action a matter of federal constitutional concern.

This last implicates a long and somewhat tangled story. If any piece of constitutional text lends itself to this fundamental shift in constitutional structure, it would seem to be the clause in the Fourteenth Amendment which provides that "No state shall make or enforce any law which shall abridge the privileges or immunities of Citizens of the United States." But, as we observed earlier in this chapter, the Privileges or Immunities Clause was the early victim of judicial hostility, and has lain dormant until its very recent invocation in a different connection in the *Saenz* case. It is a reflection of the unstoppable hydraulic force of the long-standing impulse to nationalize political justice at the state level that the judiciary simply jumped clauses, and for well more than a century has turned to the Due Process Clause of the Fourteenth Amendment instead. The why and how of this process of nationalization is an interesting and at times highly controversial chapter of constitutional history, but the outcome is stable and widely accepted: All of the guarantees of the Bill of Rights that can plausibly be understood to represent fundamental principles of political justice have been "incorporated" into the Due Process Clause of the Fourteenth Amendment. As a result, the Bill of Rights, which was originally understood to apply only to the behavior of the national government, now applies almost in full to the states and their governmental subdivisions.

Parenthetically, we should observe that what has proven to be an unstoppable march towards the enlargement of federal constitutional concern with state governmental behavior is consistent at the deepest level with the justice-seeking view of American constitutional practice. If the liberty-bearing provisions of the Constitution are understood as fixed and potentially arbitrary elements of a code laid down in the past, it is hard to see how their status could migrate from restrictions on the national government alone to restrictions on all governmental behavior. But, in contrast, if the liberty-bearing provisions of the Constitution are understood as positive-law implementations of fundamental principles of political justice, is seems only natural, indeed all but inevitable, that they would come in time to apply to all governmental behavior.

But let us return to our own line of march. Each of the Reconstruction Amendments has a clause specifically authorizing Congress to enact legislation designed to enforce the substantive provisions of that Amendment. The language of these provisions varies in trivial ways, but each gives Congress the "power to enforce" the substantive provisions of the pertinent amendment "by appropriate legislation." These provisions were not casual afterthoughts. On most tellings, it was the desire to give Congress the authority to secure the equal rights of former slaves in the wake of the Civil War that was the principal motivation for the Reconstruction Amendments. A division of constitutional labor was built into the new, post–Civil War architecture of our constitutional practice from the ground up.

The terms of that division of labor, however, remain unresolved in important respects. The nagging question posed by Congress's civil rights enforcement authority is how the scope of that authority connects with the Supreme Court's assessments of the substantive content of the implicated Amendments. It is, after all, a defining feature of the modern era of constitutional adjudication that where fundamental ingredients of political justice are at stake, the Court has typically declined to defer to legislative judgments of fact or value and has insisted on the primacy of its own all-things-considered constitutional judgment. Thus, legislative findings that certain "subversive" forms of speech pose a danger to the political community and ought to be suppressed would not without more convince the Court to permit the censorship of the implicated speech,[17] nor would legislative findings that everyone prospers best when persons of different races are educated separately have convinced the post–*Brown v. Board of Education* Court to permit the maintenance of intentionally segregated school districts. Since Congress's Section 5 authority is confined to the enforcement of the substantive provisions of the Fourteenth Amendment, and since the Court has come to insist on the primacy of its judgments with regard to the fundamental values contained in those provisions, it might seem to follow that Congress's Section 5 authority is confined to precisely those states of affairs that the Court would independently determine to be inconsistent with the substantive provisions of the Amendment.

Underenforcement enters the story at just this point. We can begin to see how this is so by considering Congress's authority under Section 2 of the Thirteenth Amendment.

JONES V. ALFRED MAYER AND REMEDIAL UNDERENFORCEMENT

Well-settled doctrine in at least one civil rights enforcement context points unmistakably in the direction of underenforcement analysis. For the past thirty years, the case of *Jones v. Alfred Mayer*[18] has defined and justified Congress's authority to legislate against private racial discrimination. In *Jones,* the Court held that Section 2 of the Thirteenth Amendment gives Congress the authority to enact sweeping protections against racially discriminatory acts by private actors in the real estate market. No Court has questioned the validity of *Jones,* and numerous congressional enactments have been expressly or tacitly upheld on its rationale. But without the conceptual assistance of the underenforcement thesis, *Jones* is deeply puzzling.

The problem is obvious: Like Section 5 of the Fourteenth Amendment and Section 2 of the Fifteenth Amendment, Section 2 of the Thirteenth Amendment gives Congress only the authority to enforce the substantive provisions of the Amendment. The Thirteenth Amendment by its terms abolishes slavery, not discrimination, and the Court has indicated a willingness to spontaneously enforce the Amendment only against actual indentured servitude, not mere discrimination.[19] How then can Congress, in the name of enforcing the Thirteenth Amendment, outlaw private discriminatory conduct?

The *Jones* Court's response to the problem of the disparity between the content it spontaneously ascribes to the Thirteenth Amendment and the range of behavior that Congress can address in the name of enforcing the Amendment is this: Congress can address not only slavery proper, but also the "badges," "incidents," and—most importantly for these purposes—the "relic(s)" of slavery. Slavery has left behind an ugly residue of entrenched bias and deprivation, and an attack on this residual injustice is within Congress's Thirteenth Amendment authority. Hence the importance of the reference in *Jones* to discrimination in housing as a "relic" of slavery: Eighty-five years earlier, a Court much less generously disposed to Congress's authority had already conceded that the "badges" and "incidents" of the grotesque institution of slavery were legitimate targets of that authority;[20] but these were understood to be the more or less contemporary extensions of slavery itself, not its lingering consequences.[21]

But the observation that Congress can address the relics of slavery as well as slavery itself is a more precise statement of the margin of the discrepancy between the scope of the Court's spontaneous enforcement of the Thirteenth Amendment and the scope of Congress's authority to enforce the same Amendment, not an explanation for that discrepancy. For that, we need underenforcement. *Jones* has to be understood as resting on the view that (1) the abolition of slavery called for in the Thirteenth Amendment implicates not just the elimination of slavery proper, but also the identification and eradication of its entrenched residue of injustice; and (2) that the Court is institutionally foreclosed from attacking the tentacular relics of slavery, but that Congress is not.

This seems an attractive view on both counts. *Jones* is the paradigm of an important and distinct group of constitutional cases, which we can call *structural harm* cases. In such cases, there is a major constitutional violation with radiant, constitutionally negative consequences. Merely stopping the unconstitutional conduct in such cases leaves a large deficit, even when measured against such goals as putting in place that state of affairs that would have obtained but for the constitutional violation. At best, structural harm cases strain the capacity of the constitutional judiciary to very near the breaking point. Judicial optimists might say this, for example, of our experience with judicial attempts to remedy school segregation and constitutionally intolerable conditions in prisons; while judicial pessimists might say we passed beyond the appropriate capacity of the judiciary in these areas.

This much should be clear: Some structural harm cases far outrun even very generous views of judicial capacity and authority. Even if we are solidly on the side of the optimists on the question of school desegregation and prison reform, it seems hard to imagine that the judiciary could go after the unhappy legacy of slavery in the United States, and, for example, invalidate any particular private act of racial discrimination or all such acts on this ground. Under these circumstances, the judiciary is obliged to stop short of anything approaching full repair of the constitutional wrong. What *Jones* does is cede to Congress the Thirteenth Amendment authority to move in the direction of completing the constitutional repair, notwithstanding the judiciary's inability to do so. This is a sensible and attractive —we might well go further and say necessary—outcome. It would be perverse to constitutional values to transfer the institutional limitations of the judiciary onto Congress under circumstances where to do so would be to guarantee a remedial shortfall.

When structural harms are as deep and as wide as those left behind by slavery and its patently unconstitutional echoes in Jim Crow laws and the segregationist practices that pervaded both the North and the South for a full century after the Civil War, there will be several curious and related features of the resulting remedial picture. First, so long as there are prominent veins of racial caste or racial subordination in our nation's social structure, we have reason to attribute this misfortune to our unconstitutional past. Second, while constitutional violations typically have a discrete and identifiable group of victims, the group of persons who continue to suffer from the pernicious residue of slavery and its aftermath is diffuse and no one person is likely to be able to establish the extent to which he or she is such a victim. Third, there are different possible strategies for addressing the entrenched consequences of our past. Some of these strategies entail costs of one kind or another; some are redundant; some are incompatible with each other; and some are simply inappropriately costly. Accordingly, it is infeasible in the extreme to stipulate that every possible measure that is likely to improve the picture must be undertaken. Fourth, there is an important and diffuse obligation which falls on at least the federal government to repair the entrenched consequences of slavery and racial discrimination; but this obligation—which we can call the *duty to repair*—does not entail a right in any given person to a particular state of affairs on the grounds that the state of affairs in question would help efface the residue of our unconstitutional past. Fifth, from all of this it follows that the duty to repair—as distinct from the duty to eradicate an extant unconstitutional practice—falls on Congress and not the constitutional judiciary.

Jones v. Alfred Mayer is a quintessential case of partnership between the Supreme Court and Congress in the enterprise of securing constitutional justice; it is also an important instantiation of the underenforcement thesis. The only wrinkle on the general theme of underenforcement in *Jones* is that here underenforcement is operating not at the level of rights definition but at the level of remedy for an acknowledged constitutional wrong.

When we go just down the block to the Fourteenth Amendment, we would expect to find much the same picture. The circumstances seem comparable. As with Section 2 of the Thirteenth Amendment, Section 5 of the Fourteenth provides that Congress can "enforce" the provisions of the Amendment by "appropriate legislation." And as with Section 2 of the Thirteenth Amendment, congressional exercises of Section 5 authority hold the promise of a more complete realization of constitutional justice. It would however, be a mistake to generalize from the approach that the Court has taken in *Jones* and its progeny. The question of Congress's authority under Section 5 is considerably more cloudy.

SECTION 5 AND REMEDIAL UNDERENFORCEMENT

Perhaps we should begin with the Section 5 problem that is most closely analogous to *Jones v. Alfred Mayer,* namely, the question of Congress's authority under Section 5 to help complete a judicially underenforced constitutional remedy for a structural harm.

On one recent occasion when a case before the Court would have been usefully analyzed in terms of underenforced constitutional remedies, no one noticed. The case was *United States v. Morrison.*[22] There, the Court invalidated a provision of the Violence Against Women Act which provided the victims of crimes of violence motivated by gender with a private cause of action against the perpetrators of such crimes. The Court held that the provisions exceeded Congress's authority under both the Commerce Clause and Section 5 of the Fourteenth Amendment.

Our present interest is the Section 5 part of the Court's analysis. That analysis was blunt: Congress's authority under Section 5 is limited to constitutional offenses defined by the substantive provisions of the Fourteenth Amendment, which address the behavior of states and state officials. The only possibly relevant violation of those provisions was the claim that in some number of states the laws protecting women against violence are not fully and successfully enforced. As to this suggested violation, the Court concluded on a variety of grounds that the creation of a cause of action against private gender-motivated violence could not plausibly be understood as a "corrective" for such ongoing state misconduct, and therefore was not within Congress's Section 5 authority.[23]

But a very different connection between the pertinent provision of the Violence Against Women Act and patent violations of the Fourteenth Amendment was available and overlooked in *Morrison*. For much of our history, women were treated in an exceptional and disabling way by the laws of every state and by those of our national government as well. Women could not vote or hold many political offices. They were excluded from diverse professions and occupations. When women married, their property rights were attributed to their husbands, and they themselves were impaired in their independent ability to engage in commercial transactions. In many instances, they were excluded from elite state educational institutions. And, of particular significance in this context, women were explicitly denied legal protection against the physical predations of their husbands. This familiar litany encompasses several centuries of what are now recognized as patent violations of the norms of constitutional equality whose textual homes are the Equal Protection Clause of the Fourteenth Amendment and the Due Process Clause of the Fifth Amendment. Like slavery, this long history of state-sponsored disablement and injustice has left behind harms that are enduring, pervasive, and tentacular. In this respect the reasoning of *Jones* is fully apt to *Morrison*. Congress's Section 5 authority to protect women from violence and discrimination is as broad as the cultural web of vulnerability to which governments at every level contributed by their plainly unconstitutional behavior. The Violence Against Women Act falls well within the scope of this remedial authority.

To be sure, this assumes that there is an ongoing vulnerability of women to violence, and further, that this entrenched vulnerability is in some meaningful part and sense attributable to our history of unconstitutional discrimination against women. Unhappily, there is no dearth of evidence to support the proposition that women are appallingly vulnerable to domestic and sexual violence.[24] In *Planned Parenthood of Southeastern Pennsylvania v. Casey*,[25] the Supreme Court had the occasion to recite at some length the findings of the District Court in that case and the findings of various other reliable sources as to the shocking exposure of women to violence from their husbands or male partners.[26] In the extensive legislative hearings that preceded the enactment of the Violence Against Women Act, Congress had before it evidence from every quarter of the widespread scourge of domestic and sexual violence in the United States, as well as evidence of the lingering attitudinal resistance to enforcing laws against such violence when it is a woman's husband, partner, or date who is the perpetrator. That evidence, in turn, was extensively rehearsed in the briefs submitted to the Court in *Morrison*, and is not open to genuine doubt.

That women's ongoing vulnerability to violence has its roots in legally endorsed historic attitudes and practices seems a matter both of common sense and common knowledge. Reflective studies of the ongoing vulnerability of women to violence point to a link of this sort. For example, two prominent researchers—Dr. Richard Gelles and Dr. Murray Straus—in their book, *Intimate Violence*, attribute the ongoing vulnerability of women to family violence to widespread social attitudes which tolerate such violence; in turn, they see those attitudes as flowing in significant part from "a centuries-old legacy in which women are men's property."[27] In this regard they highlight the "common law doctrine of coverture, under which a husband and wife took a single legal identity at marriage—the identity of the husband," and common law doctrine permitting a husband's chastisement of his wife as progenitors of contemporary attitudes.[28]

No doubt it is impossible to gauge precisely how much our history of the legal subordination of women has contributed to attitudes and reflexes that make women vulnerable now to domestic and sexual violence. Our unconstitutional regime of laws, after all, itself flowed from earlier, deeply held views about the subordination of women. But this we can know about the broad regime of unconstitutional discrimination to which women as a group were subject: That regime legitimated, amplified, and gave legal force to malign impulses, and left women more vulnerable to violence and discrimination than they would otherwise have been. That it is impossible to parse responsibility for the ongoing vulnerability of women with precision is no more a bar to Congress's authority than is the comparable observation that it is impossible to know with precision exactly how much slavery itself is causally responsible for contemporary racial injustice.

Certainly Congress had before it ample evidence of the enduring attitudinal consequences of our history of the unconstitutional treatment of women. Much of the testimony before Congress underscored the proposition that we live with a legacy of stereotypes about women's subordination to men, stereotypes that sharply contradict our best understandings of the right of women to lead secure and equal lives. In response, the Senate noted that we suffer a "legacy of societal acceptance of family violence," a legacy that "endures even today." One antecedent of that legacy specifically invoked by the Senate was the notorious common law "rule of thumb," which sanctioned the physical chastisement of wives.

Just as Congress is authorized to address the enduring and pernicious residue of slavery under Section 2 of the Thirteenth Amendment, so too our Congress has the authority to help eradicate the unhappy relics of unconstitutional gender discrimination under Section 5 of the Fourteenth; and its effort in the Violence Against Women Act to reduce the vulnerability of women to family and sexual violence should have been seen as well within the bounds of that authority.

The reader may worry that this ignores an important distinction between *Jones* and *Morrison*. Section 2 of the Thirteenth Amendment and Section 5 of the Fourteenth Amendment are textually and structurally parallel provisions, but there is this important difference: The Thirteenth Amendment is understood as barring slavery in any form and in any hands, public or private; it has no requirement of state action to overcome in the first place. In contrast, it is precisely the requirement of state action in the Fourteenth Amendment which makes Section 5 problematic as a source of authority for the private cause of action provided by the Violence Against Women Act.

But we have not ignored the problem of state action. We have from the outset assumed and insisted that violations of the Fourteenth Amendment require a delict properly assignable to a state actor; our starting point, after all, was the historical avalanche of governmental delicts with regard to gender bias. Once these constitutional wrongs have been identified, the question then becomes what is the proper scope of Congress's authority to remedy those wrongs. Congress, on this view, has authority to reach the conduct of private perpetrators of violence against women because domestic and sexual violence are in no small part triggered by attitudes and reflexes that are relics of this history of the unconstitutional treatment of women. There is no good reason to worry about the involvement of the state a second time, in the context of remedy, any more than it would have been appropriate to insist as a constitutional matter in *Jones* that racial discrimination in property transactions between private parties be deemed the equivalent of slavery.

Jones and *Morrison* both involve congressional efforts to ameliorate the lingering structural harms of historic constitutional wrongs. The structural harms of slavery and of our extensive history of official discrimination against women cannot possibly be redressed by judicial remedies alone, and this inevitable fact of judicial capacity should lead the Supreme Court to welcome Congress's partnership. This is the lesson of the underenforcement thesis—a lesson that was implicit in *Jones* and missed in *Morrison*.

The *Morrison* Court did not so much reject *Jones* and the underenforcement thesis as overlook the possibility of their applicability. For the most part, the attention of the parties and the Court was on the Commerce Clause. The parties and the numerous amici all failed to recognize the aptness of *Jones v. Mayer* and the argument from structural harm. And when the Court itself turned briefly to the question of Congress's Section 5 authority, none of the justices considered the possibility that the structural legacy of the official subordination of women was an apt target of contemporary congressional concern.

SECTION 5 AND SUBSTANTIVE UNDERENFORCEMENT

Underenforcement has a crucial substantive role as well as a remedial role to play in Section 5 analysis. Here, underenforcement has not been ignored, and here, it is as of this writing becoming the focus of an important controversy within the Court. In a series of cases dating from 1997 forward, the Court has been attracted to a model of Congress's Section 5 authority which could fairly be described as follows:

(1) For purposes of judicial decisions, at least, the Supreme Court's judgment about the meaning of the Constitution, including the Fourteenth Amendment, is authoritative;

(2) Congress's authority under Section 5 of the Fourteenth Amendment is confined explicitly to the enterprise of enforcing the substantive provisions of the Amendment;

(3) Accordingly, in evaluating legislation pursuant to that authority, the Court will insist that the enactment in question be appropriate to the enterprise of preventing or remedying what the Court would recognize as a violation of the substantive provisions of the Amendment.

If, for the moment, we imagine that the Supreme Court were in all instances taking the full measure of the substantive provisions of the Fourteenth Amendment, this is a not implausible model of Congress's Section 5 authority. There are other possible models that would be more deferential to Congressional judgment, to be sure, and those might well have substantial virtues. For example, there is a long-standing line of argument to the effect that our political structure will encourage Congress to stay within reasonable bounds in the exercise of its enumerated powers; given these incentives towards congressional self-regulation, the Court might do well to permit itself to benefit from Congress's distinct judgment at the margins of important constitutional values.

But on the hypothesis, once again, that were the Court undertaking to fully enforce the substantive provisions of the Fourteenth Amendment, there would be some virtue in the Court's insistence that Congress confine itself to reasonable remedies for what the Court would recognize as constitutional violations. The text of Section 5, after all, is clearly keyed to the substantive provisions of the Amendment, and the Court's current approach has the benefit of giving those substantive provisions the same meaning in both private right and congressional powers cases. And the Court's current approach also has the advantage of conducing to a federal division of normative labor, with Congress and the Court confined to enforcing the Constitution as interpreted by the Court, and with the states somewhat free to develop their own normative visions in the substantial space not covered by the Constitution.

All this would make the Court's current approach to Congress's Section 5 authority at least a plausible choice, were the Court fully enforcing the substantive provisions of the Fourteenth Amendment. But at exactly this point, underenforcement enters the story. Most legislation challenged on equal protection grounds is measured against the "rational basis" test. Under that test, the constitutional protagonist normally bears the burden of showing that no conceivable state of facts exists that would give the Court reason to suppose that the legislation in question bears a relationship, however attenuated, to a legitimate interest of government. As the Court itself has frequently indicated, the extravagant permissibility of this default judicial approach is in significant measure the consequence of self-conscious deference to state legislatures and to Congress.

All this is well and good—and so much a part of our modern constitutional tradition as to be considered a more or less fixed part of the doctrinal landscape. But think for a moment of exactly what widespread deference of this sort means. This is James Bradley Thayer's rule of clear mistake and then some. And it means that judges routinely let stand legislative provisions that they would adjudge to be unconstitutional were they not constrained by their role. Deference of this sort is a close cousin to the political question doctrine, and decisions which embody such deference are largely if not exclusively driven by the Court's view of its own institutional limitations, not by its analysis of the substantive requirements of the Constitution.

Under these circumstances, the simple logic of the Court's recent Section 5 decisions is inapt. Those decisions reason from the Court's insistence that its judgments of constitutional substance have primacy over those of other governmental actors to the view that Section 5 legislation must be appropriate to the enterprise of preventing or remedying what the Court would recognize as a violation of the substantive provisions of the Amendment. Where the Court's decisions are not intended to exhaust the meaning of the Fourteenth Amendment, it is in the nature of a non sequitur to limit Congress to the scope of the Court's deference-drenched Fourteenth Amendment doctrine. Unless, of course, the Court thinks that Congress is also institutionally obliged to stop far short of the full reach of the Constitution; but the Court has never suggested as much, and it is

hard to see the grounds for the Court insisting on universal deference of this sort. On the contrary, precisely because the Court is so
committed to self-restraint on institutional grounds, it should welcome the partnership of Congress in the enterprise of realizing the
values of political justice embodied in the Fourteenth Amendment.
Hence our earlier suggestion that underenforcement naturally invites a division of constitutional labor; and hence obvious concerns
about the Court's new approach to Section 5 authority, which seems
to turn a blind eye to the reality of underenforcement.

In *City of Boerne v. Flores*,[29] which launched the Court's new
approach to Section 5, the justices were preoccupied with prickly
questions about religious liberty, and the majority's Section 5 analysis went largely unexamined. In the cases immediately after *Boerne*,
questions concerning the Eleventh Amendment and the Commerce
Clause authority of Congress overshadowed the Section 5 analysis.
But in *Alabama v. Garrett*[30]—which as of this writing is the most
recent of the Court's encounters with Section 5—that section and the
question of judicial underenforcement of the Fourteenth Amendment took center stage.

In *Garrett*, a five-to-four majority held that Congress lacked
Section 5 authority to enact Title I of the Americans With Disabilities Act of 1990 (the ADA). Title I of the ADA requires employers—including state governments in their role as employers—
to "mak[e] reasonable accommodations to the known physical or
mental limitations of an otherwise qualified individual with a dis-
ability who is an applicant or employee, unless [the employer]
can demonstrate that the accommodation would impose an undue
hardship on the operation of the [employer's] business."[31] Central to
the Court's reasoning was the proposition that a state employer's
failure to accommodate the needs of a disabled job applicant or
employee would not under current equal protection doctrine constitute a violation of the Equal Protection Clause. And prominent in

the Court's discussion was the great latitude afforded governmental actors under the rational basis test.

This prompted a dissent from Justice Breyer and three of his colleagues, a dissent which sees the majority's crucial mistake as its failure to take account of the Court's chronic underenforcement of the Fourteenth Amendment:

> There is simply no reason to require Congress, seeking to determine facts relevant to the exercise of its Section 5 authority, to adopt rules or presumptions that reflect a court's institutional limitations. Unlike courts, Congress can readily gather facts from across the Nation, assess the magnitude of a problem, and more easily find an appropriate remedy. . . . Unlike courts, Congress directly reflects public attitudes and beliefs, enabling Congress better to understand where, and to what extent, refusals to accommodate a disability amount to behavior that is callous or unreasonable to the point of lacking constitutional justification. Unlike judges, Members of Congress can directly obtain information from constituents who have first-hand experience with discrimination and related issues.
>
> Moreover, unlike judges, Members of Congress are elected. When the Court has applied the majority's burden of proof rule, it has explained that we, i.e., the courts, do not "sit as a super-legislature to judge the wisdom or desirability of legislative policy determinations." . . . To apply a rule designed to restrict courts as if it restricted Congress's legislative power is to stand the underlying principle—a principle of judicial restraint—on its head. . . .[32]

Four sitting justices of the Supreme Court thus subscribe to the underenforcement thesis, and would give it bite where it matters a great deal, namely, in welcoming the collaboration of Congress in the enterprise of securing constitutional justice. But this may not be such good news, of course, since the Supreme Court glass that is four-ninths full is also five-ninths empty. Were *Garrett* best read as rejecting the idea of a collaborative division of labor in the enterprise of securing constitutional justice, it would above all be a sign of the urgency of our reflections here. We arrived at this point, remember, by asking why underenforcement matters, and we would surely find one answer here. If the contemporary Court has decisively rejected the idea that its own institutional limitations give it good cause to welcome the cooperation of Congress in securing constitutional justice, that is an error; and the underenforcement thesis explains why. But, in fact, it is too early to conclude that the Court—or indeed, any given justice in the *Garrett* majority—has turned away from the underenforcement thesis and from the possibility of a wholesome partnership between the Court and Congress in the enforcement of civil rights pursuant to Section 5 of the Fourteenth Amendment.

Imagine a justice in the *Garrett* majority who believes *both* (1) that disabled persons are not a "suspect class" within the meaning of conventional equal protection doctrine, and hence governmental conduct that puts disabled persons at a disadvantage should receive only the anemic judicial oversight of the radically deferential "rational basis" test; *and* (2) that, on the best understanding of what the Equal Protection Clause demands of government in its role as employer, disabled persons would not be entitled to the accommodation prescribed by the ADA. Nothing about a judgment that proposition (1) is true logically precludes the judgment that proposition (2) is true as well, of course; and at least two justices in the majority seem to hold exactly these views. Justices Kennedy and O'Connor joined in the majority opinion in which the rational basis test figured so prominently. But they also wrote separately to emphasize that while they applaud the ADA, violations of the Equal Protection Clause require "purposeful and intentional action" by a state. Accordingly, well-motivated failures by states to take affirmative steps like those required by the ADA could not, in their view, be construed as equal protection violations. Conspicuously, the only case Kennedy and O'Connor cite in support of their understanding of the Equal Protection Clause is *Washington v. Davis*, where the Court held that governmental entities are under no obligation to avoid actions that have a disproportionate negative impact on racial minorities.[33] They do not mention the rational basis test; on the contrary, the reader can easily draw the inference that they would have reached the same result if disabled persons were a suspect class normally entitled to "strict scrutiny."

Now, it is surely possible that the rule of *Washington v. Davis* is itself best understood as reflecting institutional concerns that lead to the underenforcement of the norms of equal protection with regard to racial minorities. After all, a requirement that governmental entities adjust their conduct to avoid disproportionate harm to such minorities, like many affirmative obligations, would carry with it concerns of strategy, responsibility and degree of the sort that argue against judicial enforcement. But Justices Kennedy and O'Connor did not ask themselves whether deference was entering their judgment through the vehicle of *Washington v. Davis*, and Justice Breyer's argument in this respect went no further than the equating of the application of the rational basis test with deference. In any event, it is entirely possible that at least two of the five justices who composed the majority in *Garrett* believed as a matter of constitutional substance *all deference aside* that a state that rationally fails to make the affirmative accommodations for disabled employees required by the ADA does not violate the Fourteenth Amendment. For any justice who holds these views, the result in *Garrett* was overdetermined; and for any justice who holds these views, judicial underenforcement of the Fourteenth Amendment is not a reason for welcoming the Americans With Disabilities Act as an exercise of Congress's Section 5 authority.

The Kennedy/O'Connor opinion in *Garrett* is important for another reason as well: It illustrates how—under some circumstances at least—a justice who has decided on grounds of judicial self-restraint not to take the full substantive measure of a provision of the Fourteenth Amendment can nevertheless determine that the provision does not reach so far as to support what purports to be an exercise of Congress's authority under Section 5 of the Amendment. For Kennedy and O'Connor, the failure of a state to accommodate special needs is, by a different name, the failure to avoid imposing a disproportionate burden on those who suffer special needs. And the obligation to avoid such an imposition, they believe, has been conclusively rejected by the Court, even with regard to racial minorities.

Given all this, *Garrett* itself is at best obscure with regard to the question of underenforcement. And none of the other cases in the *Boerne* line are any more starkly at odds with underenforcement. One other case in the line bears mention, however: In *Kimel v. Florida Board of Regents*,[34] the Court held that the Age Discrimination and Employment Act of 1967 was not within Congress's authority under Section 5. While once again the Court's opinion was replete with invocations of the rational basis test, the opinion can easily be read as rejecting the idea that considerations of age in employment—for example mandatory retirement provisions—can be thought to violate the Equal Protection Clause, all matters of deference aside. In this regard, the Court is at pains to emphasize that age is a reasonable proxy for capacity in many settings, and further, that since old age is a state to which we all destined under the best of circumstances, problems of animus or self-advantaging favoritism of the sort that breed systematic subordination are likely to be suppressed with regard to age. As with the O'Connor/Kennedy opinion in *Garrett*, the majority opinion by Justice O'Connor in *Kimel* certainly need not be read as rejecting the substantive implications for Section 5 cases of judicial underenforcement of the Fourteenth Amendment.

But our reading of *Garrett* and *Kimel* might seem to cause problems of a different sort for substantive underenforcement in Section 5 cases. The Breyer dissent in *Garrett* and the long-standing claim on behalf of the underenforcement thesis as grounds for an expansive congressional role pursuant to Section 5 depend on the existence of some cases in which the fact that the Court is underenforcing the Fourteenth Amendment matters to the Court's constitutional judgment. In effect, our reading of *Garrett* and *Kimel* depends on the view that for some of the justices in the majority, at least, a willingness to fully enforce the Equal Protection Clause would not change the substantive outcome: For these judges, neither employment decisions based on age as a reasonable proxy for capacity nor the refusal to accommodate the needs of disabled state employees would violate equal protection, even in a world of full judicial enforcement. The critical question, then, is this: Are there at least some cases where underenforcement matters to the outcome?

It seems probable that there are such cases, quite possibly an abundance of them. Consider, for example, the current provisions of the Fair Housing Act that bar discrimination based upon "familial status" and which have been interpreted as making the application of so-called "anti-grouper" municipal zoning ordinances to foster families illegal. It is entirely possible that a majority of the Court would decline to find the application of an anti-grouper ordinance to a foster home unconstitutional.

The Supreme Court has considered the application of anti-grouper ordinances in two cases. In *Village of Belle Terre v. Boraas*,[35] the Court upheld an ordinance prohibiting the occupancy of single-family homes by more than "two persons not related by blood, adoption or marriage," as applied to six graduate students living together. In *Moore v. City of East Cleveland*,[36] the Court struck down an ordinance that made it unlawful for a woman to live with her own grandchildren; but *Moore*, it should be noted, was a five-to-four decision in which the majority relied heavily on the constitutional valence of traditional familial relationships. A *Belle Terre*–type ordinance applied to a large foster family or a group home for foster children certainly seems arbitrary and unjust, but so for that matter did the ordinance in *Belle Terre* itself. Justice Douglas's opinion for the Court failed to elicit a single factual basis upon which mere occupancy by six hard-working and well-behaved graduate students threatened his romantic suburban vision of "a quiet space where yards are wide";[37] the radical deference of the rational basis test was arguably critical to the outcome. Were the Court to stand by *Belle Terre* in the face of the application of an anti-grouper ordinance to foster homes, deference to municipal judgment in local zoning matters would almost certainly be at play.

Under these circumstances, Congress should have Section 5 authority to enact legislation protecting foster families from governmental discrimination, notwithstanding judicial hesitancy in this area. Where the Court is institutionally inhibited from sympathetic evaluation of claims of constitutional injustice, it should welcome the assistance of Congress.

Hence the case for the substantive implications of the underenforcement thesis in Section 5 cases. How might the force of this claim be reflected in concrete Section 5 doctrine? The *Boerne* doctrine, as it presently stands, requires that a Section 5–based enactment be appropriate to the enterprise of preventing or remedying what the Court would recognize as a violation of the substantive provisions of the Fourteenth Amendment. Where deference is understood by the Court to play an active role in its view that a given state of affairs does not violate the Amendment, the *Boerne* approach should be modified. In areas of constitutional underenforcement, *Boerne* should be altered to embrace Section 5 legislation that is either (1) appropriate to the enterprise of preventing or remedying what the Court would recognize as a violation of the substantive provisions of the Fourteenth Amendment; or (2) appropriate to the enterprise of preventing or remedying what would be violations of rights under a plausible interpretation of the Fourteenth Amendment. For these purposes, a plausible account is one which the Court could not exclude as a possible outcome of its own judgment were its deference suspended.

We could recast this approach as an inversion of James Bradley Thayer's parable of the legislator who becomes a judge. In this inverted form, a justice of the Supreme Court who is examining the status of Section 5 legislation should ask herself whether it is plausible that if she were a member of Congress she could legitimately support the legislation as appropriate to the enterprise of preventing or remedying a violation of the Fourteenth Amendment. If the answer to that question is yes, she has good reason to uphold the legislation as an exercise of Section 5 authority. And if the answer is no, she has good reason to decline to uphold the legislation as an exercise of Section 5 authority.

A POSTSCRIPT

As this book was about to be put in its editorial bed, the Supreme Court decided *Nevada Department of Human Resources v. Hibbs*.[38] In *Hibbs*, the Court upheld the Federal Family and Medical Leave Act (FMLA) as an exercise of Congress's authority under Section 5 of the Fourteenth Amendment. The FMLA requires employers who fall under its aegis to grant employees twelve work weeks of unpaid leave each year to attend to various family-related exigencies, including the birth of a child or the serious health condition of a spouse, child, or parent. The act also provides for damages in the event that its terms are breached, and expressly includes states in the group of employers that are covered by the act and vulnerable to such actions for damages.

The Court accepted Congress's characterization of the FMLA as a remedy for discrimination against women in the workplace. The line of argument on Congress's behalf approved by the Court goes roughly like this:

(1) Among the ways in which gender discrimination in the work-place continues to be manifest is in the granting of parental and other caregiving leaves—many employers grant women such leaves but deny them to men;

(2) This perpetuates discrimination against women twice over, as it reinforces stereotypes about women as the appropriate care-givers, and discourages employers from hiring women;

(3) Merely prohibiting states and other employers from distin-guishing between men and women in leave entitlements would not be sufficient, as employers could respond by giving no leaves at all, thus excluding women—who in fact do far more caregiving than do men—from the workplace.

Hibbs's apparent embrace of Congress as a partner in the enforce-ment of the guarantees of the Fourteenth Amendment has a number of puzzling aspects. Prime among these is the Court's permitting Congress to legislate against the concern that a mere nondiscrimina-tion rule would produce a leveling down of leave opportunities and hence injure women. The problem, of course, is that—like the dis-ability accommodation requirements of the ADA in *Alabama v. Garrett*—this seems inconsistent with the Court's view that the Con-stitution permits the states to enact policies that will harm some groups disproportionately, even if those groups are constitutionally protected minorities.

But there is a strong justification for this aspect of *Hibbs*. As we noted in our discussion of *U.S. v. Morrison*, and as the *Hibbs* Court itself is at pains to emphasize, there is a long history in the United States of state-sponsored discrimination against women. If we see the ongoing disproportionate enlistment of women as family care-givers as itself a residue of that discrimination, then it makes perfect sense for Congress to require family leaves as a remedy for the structural harm of this unconstitutional past. So understood, *Hibbs* tacitly depends upon the principle of *Jones v. Alfred Mayer*; and, so understood, *Hibbs* makes perfect sense.

Seen in this light, *Hibbs* stands on a different footing than most of the earlier cases in the line spawned by *City of Boerne v. Flores*. The legacy of flagrantly unconstitutional discrimination against women cries for remedy, and that remedy must come from a legislature rather than a court. To be sure, a state employer which simply refused to grant family leaves would not be found by the Court that decided *Hibbs* to have violated the Constitution; but Congress can require family leaves precisely because the disproportionate impact on women of a no-leave policy can be seen as the residual harm of past constitutional injustices. As an Section 5 matter, accordingly, legislation addressed to the welfare of women and racial minorities should be distinctly advantaged by the echo of *Jones* in *Hibbs*.[39]

Revised Terms of Constitutional Discourse

If we see only part of the domain of constitutional justice, and take it for the whole, we can be misled. Suppose, for example, that we are considering an account of our constitutional tradition which includes but is not limited to the goal of perfecting democratic politics. Pursuant to this account, one important concern of the liberty-bearing provisions of the Constitution is the maintenance of a robust and engaged politics, a politics fully available to all citizens. Among the constitutional requirements generated by this understanding is the entitlement of all citizens to the minima of food, shelter, health care, and education necessary to making their meaningful participation in political life possible. In a conceptual world where the boundaries of the Constitution and the boundaries of constitutional adjudication are congruent, the systematic refusal of the judiciary to recognize a right to minimum welfare could loom as a significant demerit for this account of our constitutional tradition. But once underenforcement enters the story, the division of constitutional labor between courts and legislatures can be offered as an explanation for this refusal, and the general legislative commitment to basic welfare can be seen as roughly consistent with this understanding of ourselves. A judge could thus accept this enlarged process-perfecting dimension of the Constitution and act on other, judicially enforceable entailments of this understanding.

The more general implications of the underenforcement thesis for political discourse, with which we began, should not be overlooked. While it is certainly true, as we have observed, that legislators ought to consider themselves bound by principles of political justice as fully as by the Constitution, the Constitution does have a very special role in our political life. Were Congress and the President—and the Supreme Court, in the contexts we have canvassed above—to acknowledge that there is a constitutional right to minimum welfare and a constitutional obligation to repair the entrenched residue of structural injustice, the acceptance of these responsibilities in constitutional terms would have a distinct and durable impact on political perceptions.

By distinguishing the adjudicated Constitution from the full Constitution, we can make sense of our constitutional practices as a whole: We can explain the durable gap between constitutional case law and political justice, how our justice-seeking constitutional practices can ignore desperate poverty and entrenched racial and gender disadvantage. We can also explain the odd fit between generous congressional authority to enforce the Thirteenth Amendment and the far more narrow spontaneous judicial reading of that amendment, and make attractive sense out of many of the Supreme

Court's apparently anomalous engagements with the needs of the poor and the handicapped. What emerges is a picture in which we understand ourselves to be obliged—constitutionally obliged—to address the injustice of poverty and entrenched racial and gender disadvantage, but see the primary addressees of this obligation as elected officials rather than judges.

CHAPTER 8

The Domain of Constitutional Justice

The Continuing Need for Boundaries

Even after we take judicial underenforcement of the Constitution into account, there remain good reasons for supposing that the Constitution itself addresses only a subset of justice. First, a satisfactory account of our constitutional practice must recognize and respond to our durable commitment to popular political institutions, and to our durable understanding that these institutions have broad leeway in managing our political affairs. Second, part of what should give us confidence in the underenforcement thesis are the reflections in established judicial doctrine of the constitutional structure it posits: In effect, we can detect trace elements of judicially unenforceable principles in the ore of otherwise anomalous judicial doctrine. The right to minimum welfare and the obligation of redress are in this way embedded in the corpus of adjudicated constitutional law. But there are important elements of full political justice that are not similarly reflected in the corpus of constitutional law. This is true, for example, of economic justice once we leave the narrow compass of the right to minimum welfare. Third, our general sense of the realm of constitutional principle is that it is relatively narrow and relatively coherent as it stands. This sense survives the addition of important but judicially unenforceable constitutional norms like the right to minimum welfare and the obligation to reform entrenched bias; but other possibilities—like the obligation to pursue full economic justice—seem to fit poorly with the extant mix.

Very few constitutional observers believe that the Constitution requires perfect economic justice, whatever that might be. This is no small enclave around which the Constitution skirts: The area left untouched is a catch-all that includes just about every aspect of distributive justice that is not marked by the extreme and enduring vulnerability of a limited set of victim groups. The right of minimum welfare and the obligation to redress entrenched bias seem to fit with the limited set of distributive concerns recognized by the Constitution precisely because they deal with the extremity of circumstance faced by the victims of grinding poverty or entrenched bias. Debates on the frontier of constitutional law—like the question of the rights of homosexuals to be free from discrimination—do not put this basic shape of the Constitution's concerns at contest; rather, they are debates about whether the circumstances that surround homosexuality in our culture conform to the limited range of the Constitution's concerns. Outside a small handful of cases of special vulnerability, distributional matters of every kind, touching on matters ranging from the use of one's land to the use of one's time and work in a profession, to the apportionment of taxes and the disgorgement of public benefits—all are matters in the capacious category of economic justice, left untouched by constitutional constraint.

What stops our constitutional tradition from pressing ahead into some or all of these questions?

It might be tempting to answer that constitutional justice implicates only the behavior of government, and that the salient features of our economic arrangements are private. But, as the Court in *Shelley v.*

Kraemer[1] famously discovered, there is a conceptual continuum between that which the state actively does, that which it endorses, and that which it merely tolerates. In economic matters in particular we understand that the extant distribution of wealth and opportunity is critically connected to the state's regime of law, to the decisions explicitly or tacitly made by state actors in their solemn official capacities.[2] There are, of course, matters so private that a constitution should protect them from its own reach as well as the reach of legislation and common law supervision, as a matter of justice. This is neither paradoxical nor particularly hard to grasp. But that is not the view we take of our economic arrangements. Our repudiation of the tradition of *Lochner v. New York*[3] was not based on the idea that economic transactions are beyond the reach of the Constitution, but on the insistence that the state can pursue a variety of economic approaches and employ a wide range of economic regulatory mechanisms, without transgressing constitutional constraints.

The underenforcement thesis takes us some distance towards understanding the limited scope of the adjudicated Constitution, but this sweeping truncation of constitutional justice goes considerably deeper than the question of judicial enforcement. We are, therefore, back to the question of the domain of constitutional justice itself. Indeed, when we recognize that adjudication does not exhaust the authoritative reach of the Constitution, the enterprise of identifying the distinct domain of constitutional justice becomes both more difficult and more useful. If the adjudicated Constitution were the whole of the Constitution, there would then be two immediate guides to the boundaries of constitutional justice: The pattern of adjudication over time would offer a good picture of this domain for us to interpret; and insights about the limits of judicial competence would offer a conceptual basis for the drawing of that domain's boundaries. When we admit underenforcement into the picture, our inquiry is more difficult. It also more useful, of course: An understanding of the reach of constitutional justice will be an important guide to the content of the judicially unenforceable portion of the Constitution.

All this leaves us with a rather complex picture of constitutional justice. Constitutional justice sits between all of political justice, on the one hand, and the much narrower substance of the adjudicated Constitution on the other. We can expect constitutional justice to draw from political justice and to be reflected in turn in the substance of the adjudicated Constitution, but it occupies its own domain, narrower than the former and broader than the latter. The conceptual boundaries of that domain are the object of our inquiry.

Democratarian Accounts and the Domain of Constitutional Justice

There is a somewhat common modern view of our constitutional practice which accepts—and indeed, depends upon—the idea that there is a domain of constitutional justice of the sort we are after. A number of commentators see the project of constitutional justice as that of perfecting democracy, of bringing our public institutions and projects closer to the democratic ideal. These theories span a substantial range of ideas about just how demanding the ideal form of democracy is. John Hart Ely's well-known treatment of this theme in his book *Democracy and Distrust*[4] is often characterized as majoritarian, and indeed it does emphasize the procedural dimensions of democracy, including and especially freedom of expression and the satisfactory alignment of the franchise, broadly understood. Even Ely, however, is anxious to defend the centerpiece of the Warren Court's constitutional lessons, the protection of African Americans against discriminatory treatment; this important substantive commitment does not comfortably fit Ely's process-based understanding of the domain of the Constitution. Still, Ely's attachment to process has real consequences in his theory. The possibility of constitutional autonomy—for example, the recognition in *Griswold v. Connecticut*[5] of a right to privacy broad enough to protect married persons' decisions to buy and use contraceptive devices—does not enjoy a place at Ely's democracy-perfecting table. At the other end of the spectrum is Ronald Dworkin.[6] His idea of constitutional democracy is keyed to the question of what circumstances make it possible for self-determination in the personal sense to co-exist with self-determination in the public, democratic sense. The result is an account of democracy which is broad, and encompasses many substantive features, including any aspect of individual autonomy Dworkin might otherwise be tempted to award constitutional status. Somewhere between Ely and Dworkin is (or at least, at one point was) Frank Michelman, who argued that some claims for autonomy—like the right to openly pursue one's gay sexual orientation—are connected to the improvement of democracy because they make it possible for citizens to find and fulfill their true identities, and hence participate more authentically as citizens in the political process.[7]

As a corollary to their insistence that the domain of constitutional justice is confined to the improvement of the conditions of democracy, these *democratarian* accounts of our constitutional practice claim for themselves a particular conceptual advantage. They claim to significantly ameliorate, or even eliminate, the tension between our constitutional practice and democracy. If the job of the Constitution and our constitutional institutions is to improve the circumstances of democracy, democratarian theorists argue, then they can hardly be faulted on the grounds that they are undemocratic. Judicial intervention in the name of democracy is pro-democratic, not counter-democratic. This putative advantage of democratarian accounts of the Constitution, in fact, is often offered as an important reason for identifying the improvement of democracy as the exclusive domain of constitutional justice.

Democratarian accounts have considerable intuitive appeal. They also have a number of difficulties. We will consider their liabilities first, and then consider what sustains their appeal. We can begin by observing that the conceptual judo of these accounts, which seem to turn the force of democratic objections to robust adjudication against themselves, is much overstated. To see why this is so, let us consider a spectrum of political states of affairs, running from a radically deficient state, democratic in form only, at one end to a perfect democracy at the other. When the affairs of a political community are sufficiently close to the awful end of this spectrum, there is little or no reason to prefer the results from the badly deformed popular process, simply because it has the form of a majoritarian institution, over the studied judgment of the constitutional judiciary. Fair enough. But at some point along the spectrum, moving towards the ideal end, there will be a point where political arrangements satisfy the requirements of what we might call a working democracy: The franchise is reasonably well distributed, the channels of political expression are open, and there is no gross distortion of the political process. At this point, there could be real cost in displacing the judgments of the ordinary political process. From this point forward, progress towards the ideal is likely to be controversial among well-intentioned observers; the judiciary may surely be making what it regards as improvements in democracy, but reasonable persons may well disagree; and the question will become who should decide what qualifies as an improvement in democracy. Now, the voice of the people speaking through reasonably well-formed popular political institutions has a claim to authority that cannot be dismissed out of hand.

By most accounts, we in the United States are a working democracy. The constitutional judiciary plays an important role in our political life as a justice-seeking mechanism and can be defended—indeed welcomed—on that ground; but judicial intervention in the name of the Constitution is not necessarily cost-free in the way that democratarian theorists suggest, even if the judiciary confines itself to the enterprise of improving the democratic process.

Or perhaps it would be more accurate to say this: If judicial intervention in the name of the Constitution is cost-free, it is not cost-free for the reason that democratarian theorists give. I offer this alternative formulation because I think that the view that some cost is paid whenever an important public decision is taken out of the hands of the popular political process is itself doubtful. We do not think that there is cause for regret, without more, in the fact that we as a political community treat the shape of our basic political institutions as settled, and normally decline to actively revisit historical choices with regard to these institutions. It seems wrong to say that this is because we gain more in terms of stability and efficiency than we lose in terms of democratic choice; the point rather is that there is no loss in generally conceding these decisions to history. Similarly, if a democratic people live with a set of political institutions and practices that include a justice-seeking constitution and a responsible constitutional judiciary, it is far from clear that there is even a prima facie cost in terms of democratic choice. If there is a broad popular domain in which choices are made by reasonably well-designed popular political institutions, and a constitutional domain in which an important but narrow set of precepts of political justice are well tended by a robust judiciary, there may be no such loss. This is a matter of some complexity, and we will defer our discussion of it until chapter 10. The important point is that democratarian judicial restraint is not the talisman: If there is a cost in placing constitutional choices in the hands of the transtemporal partnership between founding generations and judges, democratarian restraint does not cancel it; alternatively, if there is no such cost, democratarian restraint is not the reason.

By putting so much emphasis on an open-textured concept like democracy as the lamp for the constitutional genie, democratarian accounts are prone to distortion in one of two offsetting directions. If the concept of democracy is held stable and relatively narrow, democratarian accounts truncate the reach or distort the motivation of constitutional justice; hence the idea that gays and lesbians owe their right to live within their deep sexual identities to their ultimate service as voters, or even that they have no such right at all. Alternately, democratarian accounts can put inappropriate weight on artful understandings of the requirements of democracy, and create the sense that democracy is being used as the shell for claims of justice that belong elsewhere, or at least that too much is being made to turn on whether a particular, perfectly attractive claim of justice is inside or outside democracy as appropriately understood.

But democratarian accounts have considerable appeal, and we can learn from them. Part of what makes them attractive is the sense, latent in their insistence on democracy as the object of constitutional justice, that the Constitution is meant to prepare the field and set the ground rules for popular politics, not replace those politics as the primary mechanism of policy choice in American government. But understood in this way, democracy is merely a placeholder for this basic sense. Even as democratarian accounts remind us that constitutional justice should play this general role in our political life, they mislead by equating that insight with stipulation that only that which composes democracy is a proper object of constitutional attention.

Democratarian accounts are attractive for two other reasons, both particularly congenial to our inquiry. First, democratarian accounts proceed from a justice-seeking view of our constitutional practice: Democracy enters the democratarian story in the right way, as part of a reflection on the question of what understanding of the liberty-bearing provisions of the Constitution will best serve political justice; and even comparatively bare-bones democratarians like John Hart Ely insist that there must be considerable room for the independent, justice-seeking judgment of constitutional judges. Second, democratarian accounts do not posit arbitrary or happenstantial limits to the scope of constitutional justice; they point to limits that can be explained with regard to the Constitution as a whole, and more generally, with regard to the role of a constitution in a liberty-loving political community. Democratarian accounts describe and undertake to defend constitutional justice as committed to a subset of the principles of political justice; they point to a domain of constitutional justice in the stronger sense that we named as our goal at the outset of this inquiry.[8]

The Burdens of Membership in a Political Community

So we turn at last to sketch the domain of constitutional justice. I propose that we begin by considering what would worry persons like those who shaped the founding and the refounding (or the completion of the founding represented by the Reconstruction Amendments) of our Constitution—what the most urgent fears of the soon-to-be-members of our political community would have been. This may seem a benign enough starting point, but even this modest formulation of the question raises some difficulties that we would do well to address at the outset.

When we set out to determine the domain of constitutional justice, our inquiry straddles the local and the global. On the one hand, we are trying to understand our Constitution and our constitutional practices and the question of the domain of constitutional justice is in this way inspired by, particular to, and subject to the limitations of our constitutional experience. On the other hand, what we wish to know is whether our constitutional commitments connect in a nonarbitrary way to what makes constitutions valuable to political societies in general, and what makes ours valuable to us in particular. We can answer that question (even in its more particularized form) only by making judgments about what makes a constitution valuable to a people like us, who value the core elements of political justice—to a people, that is, who value democracy, equality, and liberty. A successful account of our constitutional practice, accordingly, will necessarily draw our attention to universal features of constitutionalism, and, it is to be hoped, will inform not only persons interested in evaluating and shaping our constitutional institutions but those whose concerns are with the direction of constitutional development in other countries. The local/global dualism of our inquiry is reflected in the form of the question I have just put, which asks after the concerns of persons *like* those who shaped the founding of our Constitution.

Asking what would urgently worry persons joining a political community may seem an oddly constricted and negative lens through which to approach the question of the domain of constitutional justice. After all, people who form or reform political communities have many positive hopes and ambitions, ambitions for a more perfect—read peaceful and prosperous—union. They want their government to make wise and decisive choices, to conduct itself effectively in international affairs, to successfully manage the domestic economy, and so on. All this was certainly true of the persons who founded our constitutional community. And while their diverse concerns may come freighted with greater or lesser passion and urgency, there is no reason to suppose that they parked their lesser concerns at the Constitution's door.

But our concern is with constitutional *justice*. In general, justice is concerned most clearly and centrally with avoiding various nasty states of affairs—prominent failures to treat individuals and groups fairly. This focus on the negative and further, on the urgently negative, is especially apt to *constitutional* justice. Constitutional precepts need to be durable, spare, and capable of reasonably clear application and judgment; constitutional justice, accordingly, should narrow its focus to extreme and rather clear breaches of political justice.

The need for the Constitution to speak with a parsimonious, focused clarity may not be obvious, especially in a conceptual environment that recognizes that the judicially enforced portion of the Constitution does not exhaust the whole. If we were operating on the understanding that the judiciary is empowered and obliged to enforce the whole of the Constitution, there would be a more obvious need for constitutional parsimony, since to place a matter under the aegis of the Constitution would be to commend it to the authority of the constitutional judiciary, and we have already encountered good reasons for thinking that some aspects of political justice are not well suited to judicial enforcement. Having thus acknowledged the limits of the judicially enforced Constitution, why should we also narrow the focus of the Constitution itself?

There are two important and closely related reasons for maintaining a narrowed constitutional focus. First, while we have been at pains to resist the democratarian impulse to confine constitutional justice to the limits of a stipulated conception of democracy, no one can doubt that a comparatively robust commitment to democratic rule is an important part of political justice in general and of constitutional justice in particular. Constitutional justice thus carries the seeds for its own substantive restraint, since the concern for democracy insists that whatever values of constitutional justice lie outside democracy not unduly congest the field over which democratic choice can operate.

This concern obviously extends to those political decisions that are *preference-driven,* that is, to those questions—like the choice between museums and playing fields—where the best answers are constituted or at least importantly inflected by the distribution of preferences among the members of our political community. Less obviously, perhaps, but no less importantly, the concern for democratic choice also extends to many questions that are *judgment-driven*—questions where the best answers are constituted by concerns of justice independent of the distribution of preferences, and where the best answers hopefully are chosen rather than constituted by the weight of popular judgment. Thus, for example, decisions about the environmental legacy of our generation, or the perpetuation of the national debt, or the waging of morally contestable wars may be properly understood as judgment-driven, but they belong to the people, not to the Constitution. It bears emphasis that democracy enters our story here not as distinct from or prior to constitutional justice, but rather as an important—albeit nonexclusive—requirement of constitutional justice itself.

The second reason for maintaining a narrowed constitutional focus is more overtly pragmatic. Suppose we were able to agree—more or less—on the underlying principles of distributive justice applicable to a modern society. Even given this heroic assumption, there would remain staggering issues of strategy, priority, and timing. Imagine that we have something like a comprehensive picture of the way in which our society—now and projected forward in time—fails to satisfy the requirements of distributive justice. That picture is going to suggest an enormous range of hard choices. Whose legitimate complaints do we address first: The worst off, or the larger group (we imagine) who are quite badly but not worst off? By what arbitrage do we adjust the unrequited claims of present members of our political community against the competitive claims (again, we imagine) of members yet to be born? Fundamental structural features of our economy—for example, whether it is market-driven or centrally managed—and fundamental directions of culture and enterprise—for example, whether we are to be an agrarian or industrial society—will have immediate and long-term consequences for distributive justice; these fundamental features and directions also have enormous consequences on many other fronts. To what degree does distributive justice govern or prevail against other strong reasons we have for making these fundamental choices? When and to what degree is it appropriate to defer present justice in favor of greater future justice? These are just an arbitrary few of the questions that flood forward even after agreement on basic principles. The picture, I mean to suggest, is like the game of *Go*, exaggerated many times over and in many dimensions: In *Go*, there are many small skirmishes all over the board between the protagonists; the great difficulty for each player is in choosing where to fight and for how long.

And this dizzying picture, bear in mind, is drawn on the hypothesis that we could reach broad agreement on the underlying principles of distributive justice applicable to a modern society. These principles, even in the abstract, are notoriously open to disagreement. They are also unusually prone to confusion of a particular sort, namely, the confusion between basic and enduring principles and more transitory or passing concerns that may connect for a time with, and be mistaken for, those deeper precepts.

The point is emphatically not that conscientious political decision-makers should ignore the broad concerns of justice; the point is that to be effective, a constitution must be more focused and more insistent than general principles of justice which by their nature are radically open to contest, offset, and temporizing. A constitution can significantly enhance political judgment over the concerns of justice only if it restricts itself to demands so basic and so durable that they can generally and reasonably function as dominant and nonnegotiable. This, if anything, is the more true of constitutional precepts that elude judicial enforcement. If the judicially unenforced portions of our Constitution were swamped with the broad and undifferentiated concerns of distributive justice it would lose the capacity to offer a firm and unduckable basis for challenge and debate.

We can see the important connection between these two points by considering an objection that could be raised to the first. The objection goes as follows: Surely all political choices should acknowledge the demands of justice, broadly conceived; democracy does not imply a freedom from responsible judgment; accordingly, there can be no democratic harm in calling all the requirements of justice "constitutional," as long as that fable does not always imply that the judiciary is entitled to second-guess the "constitutional" decisions of popular political entities.

But this objection overlooks the interaction of the claim from democracy with the claim from constitutional efficacy. The bite— the value and real-world significance—of judicially unenforced constitutional rights depends upon a variety of related circumstances. First, it is important that the judiciary be able to police such rights at their substantive, procedural, and institutional margins. Second, in order both to enable this policing and to meaningfully guide popular political choice, it is important that judicially unenforced constitutional rights be recognizably of a piece with the adjudicated Constitution. And third, it is important, as we have been at pains to emphasize, that judicially unenforced constitutional rights be able to speak with what at least approaches uncompromising authority over the competing concerns of our political community. By now the reader may have guessed where this is leading: If judicially unenforced constitutional rights acquire significance as a result of their categorical authority, oneness with the material of the adjudicated Constitution, and reinforcement by the judiciary in its role as supporting political actor, then they will constrict democratic choice. That, after all, is precisely what we would hope of them.

Only by restricting itself to urgent and nonnegotiable requirements that are fundamentally of a piece with the articulate principles of the adjudicated Constitution can the judicially unenforced Constitution deliver on the promise of being the durable conscience of democratic politics. Hence the need for triage, for focusing on the most urgent concerns of political union.

So, to the worries of persons like those who shaped our Constitution: For the members of any political community there is the certainty that some questions of considerable importance will be decided against their interests. That is the situation even in a democracy, of course, where someone has to lose elections and lose votes in the legislative assembly. No political community can avoid the prospect of disappointment, and that is an important part of what potential members of a community must consider when contemplating the structure of that community. Disappointment for these purposes includes not just failures to prevail as to goals, priorities, and strategies on matters of public policy, but various burdens of membership that may be unjust or oppressive. Membership will always entail burdens, even for those who do prevail; this is true, for example, of reasonable taxes levied in pursuit of the very projects that one has sponsored or endorsed. But the burdens of membership will not always be welcome in this way, or reasonable. They have the potential to be of such magnitude or so constricting of individual choice as to radically diminish the quality of one's life.

This point is sometimes sharpened and redirected by a play on words. The problem for a democracy, it is sometimes said, is how to reconcile two states of affairs, both of which are highly esteemed: self-rule (or self-determination) in the sense of an individual's control over her own life, and self-rule (or self-determination) in the group sense of democratic rule. The two are obviously in tension. Every individual gives up some control to the political community of which she is a part, even in the best of circumstances; and the democratic insistence on self-government at the group level seems to imply the absence of precisely the sort of restraint or intervention in the majoritarian process that is required to preserve important elements of individual self-rule. Those who are inclined to see the problem in these terms are apt to offer solutions of the form: If the members of a political community have the proper relationship to their community, it is appropriate to regard their individual choices as subsumed within the group choices of the community as a whole.

There are several respects in which this seems to make the problem too fine, and the solution too grand. Self-government in the personal sense is never anything like fully possible. We simply cannot all be dictators to the whole, and many of us will fail to prevail with regard to some or even many public decisions, some or many of which in turn will be important to us. There surely is an important connection between self-rule writ small for the individual and large for the community: If individuals within a community do not in some meaningful sense enjoy the capacity to reflect upon and choose among values, commitments, and projects for themselves and their community, then it is hard to see why "self-determination" at the community level is a meaningful or valuable commodity; conversely, the capacity to maintain one's independence is surely prominent among the conditions that make the burdens of membership tolerable. But it is not the case that the disappointments or burdens of membership can be made to disappear, that the individual can be made to own or identify with the decisions of the group in such a way that no disparity in interest or concern between the group and the individual exists. Neither is it the case that protecting individual choice against group domination is the only legitimate and urgent concern about the burdens of group membership.

Justifying and constraining the disappointments and burdens of membership in a political community is the crucial project of constitutional justice. Under the circumstances of the constitutional founding and refounding of our political community, this project was of particular importance. (We should note, however, that this is a common feature of constitutional foundings.) At the Founding, the transfer of a substantial but necessarily unknown degree of governmental authority from the states to the national government was the occasion for sharp attention by a plural people to constitutional constraints on the burdens of membership. Membership in the national political community involved giving over potentially significant aspects of one's welfare and destiny to a national process of political choice over which one's friends and family could exert only limited influence. Hence the firm insistence on a national government of limited powers, on the state-centered composition of the Senate, and, ultimately, on a Bill of Rights preoccupied with liberty-bearing restraints on the national government.

During Reconstruction, the structure of constitutional concern was different, but the basal substance of that concern was not. Now the project was that of extending true membership in our political community to those who had borne the grotesque burdens of slavery and of placing the responsibility and authority for securing the privileges and immunities of that membership into the hands of the only government that seemed trustworthy in the service of that undertaking. It was, accordingly, the distribution rather than the terms of membership that was the primary focus of the Reconstruction Amendments.

What should persons in the circumstances of those who founded and refounded our political community have been at pains to secure through the mechanism of their constitutional arrangements in order to constrain and justify the burdens and disappointments of membership in our political community? I think that each person or group in our political community has good reason to insist on these four broad concerns: first, that their interests and concerns be treated with the same respect as the interests and concerns of all other groups and persons (we can call this equal membership);

second, that the processes of government be fair to them and open to their participation and voice (we can call this fair and open government); third, that matters in the community be so arranged as to offer them the opportunity to secure materially decent lives (we can call this the opportunity to thrive); and fourth, that they have the opportunity to form judgments about their lives and the government under which they live their lives, and reasonable latitude in leading the lives they choose to lead (we can call this independence).

Equal membership, fair and open government, the opportunity to thrive, and independence. These are the basic, urgent concerns of political membership for a plural people whose life projects are at once important to them and the source of much of their plural division. These concerns are not meant to be read as immediate propositions of constitutional justice. The pursuit of some substantive principles (like the principle of free speech and its entailments) is demanded by these concerns, and some institutional arrangements (like particular distributions of authority across branches or between federal layers) may be favored by them. But these concerns are signposts to the neighborhood of constitutional justice; they describe its domain, not its axiomatic content.

It may be useful to compare this characterization of the domain of constitutional justice with the idea of political legitimacy. Views about the preconditions of a legitimate government vary considerably, so this is a bit of a moving target. Still, these observations may help: If legitimacy is taken seriously and literally, it has to be understood to comprise rather weak conditions, lest the vast bulk of world governments past and present be pronounced illegitimate; we may need to save that unhappy verdict for extreme cases. Full realization of each of the concerns within the domain of constitutional justice may thus be a standard more demanding than political legitimacy; but, if so, this is more a matter of the frailty of our (species-wide) capacity to make and abide by satisfactory collective arrangements and commitments than it is a case of setting our constitutional sights too high. As a bottom line: No modern government could legitimately renounce any one of these concerns; the failure of a government to meet these concerns fully, while possibly inevitable, is nonetheless deeply regrettable; and the chronic and blatant failure to meet any one of these concerns should cast doubt on the legitimacy of the government in question.

Our Constitution—and we can expect this of constitutions generally—is in this sense aspirational but not utopian. The Constitution aims not at a hopelessly artificial state of perfection, but at a not fully obtainable state in which the most critical, baseline demands of political justice are met. If men and women were angels, we would not need governments; and if governments were fundamentally just we would not need constitutions.

These concerns clearly do not exhaust the requirements of political justice. We could imagine states of affairs, for example, that fully satisfied the requirement that circumstances in the political community be so arranged as to give each member of the community the opportunity to live a materially decent life, but which fell significantly short of a just allocation of opportunity and resources.

I have not offered an extended defense of these four concerns here, but I expect them to be generally well received, in light of our actual constitutional experience (about which more will be said in the next section), and in light of our common instincts about what it is that wary members of a political community would and should worry about. I imagine, however, that readers may have doubts about the opportunity to thrive, which can be described as the opportunity of hard-working persons to provide themselves and their families with decent material lives.

Complaints, I think, could come in two flavors. First, the objection might be that the insertion of material well-being into the list of the urgent concerns about the disappointments and burdens of political membership requires a special defense. Second, the objection might be that the kind and level of the material well-being stipulated by the opportunity to thrive seems inappropriately arbitrary, or simply wrong.

The inclusion of some concern for material well-being is not hard to justify, either as a general concern of membership in a political community or in the particular circumstances of the Founding and Reconstruction. Our revolution, like most revolutions, was prompted in significant part by economic injustices—consider "taxation without representation." Ours was an economic Constitution, with the amalgamation of the states into an open and unified national economic regime being high or highest on the list of reasons for replacing the Articles of Confederation. Unsurprisingly, the principal divisions at the Constitutional Convention were closely associated with concerns for the material circumstances of economic life. During Reconstruction, the prosperity of the emancipated slaves was an important part of the concerns for justice in the Fourteenth Amendment, with the national legislation retroactively authorized by the Amendment conspicuously granting equal rights to contract and to hold and enjoy real property, and with the Amendment itself announcing concern for deprivations of property without due process of law. So too, modern civil rights legislation has been heavily preoccupied with material well-being, attacking discrimination in housing, employment, and education. There is nothing unique about the materiality of these constitutional events. We would be astonished to learn that a new constitution in South Africa, or Latin America, or Eastern Europe had been enacted without serious attention to economic concerns.

The more serious complaint is that I have arbitrarily and conveniently given the constitutional concern for material well-being the particular size and shape of the opportunity to thrive. Why for example, not insist on broad economic justice, or stipulate the rough content of economic justice in a manner consistent with our long-standing commitment to a market economy, or demand something like the opportunity to prosper according to one's talents and capacities? Or why not read into constitutional justice a general predisposition to Locke and his proviso? Or why not see only a concern with certain forms of pernicious discrimination? Why this moderate and vague opportunity to lead a materially decent life?

The complaint that the opportunity to thrive is an arbitrary cut at the material dimension of constitutional justice, could, in turn, rest on one of three different claims. The first form of the objection would deny that the opportunity to thrive is itself a part of or is subsumed within the critical material requirements of political justice. The second form of the objection would deny that the opportunity to thrive is appropriately concrete and immediate in its entailments to qualify as a constitutional concern. The third form of the objection would agree that the material dimension of constitutional justice should in one way or another encompass the opportunity to thrive, but would argue for inclusion in the constitutional canon of more robust (and possibly more philosophically complete) requirements of distributional justice.

The view that political justice does not include the opportunity to thrive simply is not plausible. To be locked in grinding poverty is an awful form of human existence. For those who suffer that state, the promise of equal membership, fair and open government, and independence are empty and meaningless. A society that organizes its affairs in a way that fails to provide the opportunity to thrive can hardly have regarded the interests of those who lack such an opportunity with the same respect as the interests and concerns of other groups and persons (equal membership); in no meaningful sense are the processes of government fair to persons who are locked in poverty, or open to their participation and voice (fair and open government); and no group has less of an opportunity to form judgments about their lives and the government under which they live their lives, and less latitude in leading the lives they choose to lead (independence). For a prosperous society in normal times—even for a society deeply wed to free markets as, inter alia, the basis of that prosperity—it cannot be just to maintain economic arrangements that fail to provide its citizens with the opportunity to thrive.

The suggestion that the opportunity to thrive is not appropriately shaped to qualify as a constitutional requirement—that it is not sufficiently concrete and immediate to be effective in this role—appeals to our earlier observation about the need for parsimonious clarity in constitutional precepts. In thinking about this objection, we must observe two distinctions: The first is between a concern within the domain of constitutional justice itself and the more precise principles or precepts that the concern may sponsor or entail; the second is between the question of whether a principle or precept is enforceable by the judiciary and the question of whether it is sufficiently urgent, concrete, and focused to function as an immediate, more or less nonnegotiable demand of constitutional conscience.

With these distinctions in mind, let us consider the right to minimum welfare which we defined earlier as the entitlement of members of our political community to economic arrangements that offer them minimally decent material lives in exchange for hard work on their own behalf. The right to minimum welfare, as we discussed, is not enforceable by the judiciary in a full and direct sense (although the judiciary can and does police it at its substantive and procedural margins); it is, however, urgent, concrete, and focused. In a prosperous political community that recognizes the right to minimum welfare as a requirement of justice, the right has the right shape and form to function as a more or less nonnegotiable demand of constitutional conscience.

The right to minimum welfare is somewhat narrower and more precise than the opportunity to thrive, which we described as the requirement that matters in a political community be arranged so as to offer the community's members the opportunity to secure materially decent lives. This reflects a certain tension latent in our analysis to this point that I would like to take a moment to discuss directly. On the one hand, I have suggested that the concerns that compose the domain of justice are more basic and general than would be the operative principles—the axioms and postulates, if you will—of a scheme of constitutional justice. In this vein, I have talked about the entailments of these concerns. We could not, for example, treat seriously the concern for fair and open government without a commitment to a robust principle of free expression, and we could not treat seriously the concern for the opportunity to thrive without a commitment to the right to minimum welfare. On the other hand, I have suggested that a principle of parsimony attaches to the domain of constitutional justice because, to be effective, a constitution must make immediate and essentially nonnegotiable demands. The reader might well wonder whether and why the more general concerns that compose the domain of justice have to be limited if it is the entailments of these concerns that are operational, that have to do the categorical work.

The point is this: Our central inquiry in these pages is about the shape of the domain of constitutional justice and its justification. That shape, I have argued, is best understood as reflective of the most urgent and durable concerns of the members of a political community. The liberty-bearing facets of a constitution need to be so confined, in important part, because only then can the constitution function appropriately and effectively as the political conscience of an ongoing democratic community. In practice, this means that the concerns taken up by a constitution must give on to substantive constitutional principles that have the right sort of bite.

"Must give on to" is an intentionally soft phrase. Roughly, I have this in mind: A constitutional concern should clearly point towards one or more operational constitutional principles, compliance with which would go a substantial distance towards the satisfaction of the underlying concern. A well-shaped and robust doctrine of free speech, for example, would be part of a set of operational principles, which, if complied with, would go a substantial distance towards satisfying the underlying concern of fair and open government; the right to minimum welfare bears this same relationship to the opportunity to thrive.

Finally, let us consider the third form of the complaint that the opportunity to thrive represents an arbitrary cut at the material requirements of political justice. This form of the complaint agrees that the material dimension of constitutional justice should in one way or another encompass the opportunity to thrive, but argues for inclusion in the constitutional canon of more robust requirements of distributional justice. In responding, I want to agree that it is neither crucial to my analysis nor possible to defend the precise formulation of either the opportunity to thrive or the right to minimum welfare.[9] Still, there are important advantages to these or to roughly comparable formulations; a review of those advantages will not only explain my formulation but suggest what would make alternative formulations roughly comparable.

First, there is the point upon which we rested earlier: To be effective, constitutional concerns have to embody or give on to durable, concrete, gripping, essentially nonnegotiable claims of constitutional conscience; broad commitments to economic justice of many stripes will flunk this requirement. Second, as we will see more fully in the next section, our constitutional tradition displays trace elements of a right to minimum welfare of the modest sort I have proposed; a significantly more robust right of material well-being would not be able to claim fit with our tradition. Third, the four concerns of constitutional justice that we have identified must be read in relation to each other. Equal membership, fair and open government, and independence are consistent with the opportunity to thrive and its instantiation in the right to minimum welfare; indeed, they require the satisfaction of the right to minimum welfare for their own fulfillment. But a significantly more robust concern for material well-being as a constitutional precept might well be inconsistent with the confluence or union of these other concerns. Thus, for example, the diversity of life projects characteristic of a plural society which respected these nonmaterial concerns will require democratic contests about conflicting courses of economic development. Fourth, flexibility in the arrangement of the economy is crucial to prosperity over time, and a concern for material well-being in an enduring constitution needs to be appropriately adaptable; the opportunity to thrive and the right to minimum welfare it brings with it leave most of the details of the economy unspecified and are themselves softly indexed to prevailing expectations and material circumstances.

The Domain of Constitutional Justice and Our Constitutional Tradition

Does this description of the domain of constitutional justice fit our actual constitutional experience? What we have described as making up the domain of constitutional justice are four interrelated concerns. It does not count as a demerit on grounds of fit that there is no simple, straightforward correspondence between these concerns and the specific clauses of the Constitution or the formal conceptual structure of constitutional doctrine. The question is whether the jurisprudence of the liberty-bearing features of our constitutional tradition can be fairly understood as reflecting the urgent pull of these basic concerns.

The point that there need be no one-to-one or nominal correspondence between the concerns that make up the domain of constitutional justice and the textual or doctrinal packages of our liberty-bearing constitutional tradition for there to be a good fit between that tradition and the domain of constitutional justice requires some elaboration. The reader may worry that I have ignored an important distinction between the content and the purposes of a constitution. We can imagine, for example, a constitution that by its terms addressed only the durable, structural features of government, and made no textual reference to principles of liberty or equality. We can imagine further that the constitutional judiciary has read this "constitution lite" as raising only questions of governmental structure, but that, in resolving such questions, the judiciary invokes the ideas of liberty and equality as important among the goals of the constitution's structural stipulations, and therefore as important guides to the best interpretation of those stipulations. Under these circumstances, ideas of political justice would figure in the best understanding of the constitution as the purposes against which its interpretation should be judged, but they would not be part of the constitution; they would operate at an instrumental remove from the substance of the constitution. If the connection between the concerns that make up the domain of constitutional justice and the substance of our constitutional tradition were like that, then of course there would be a discontinuity between the two. If the connection were like that, however, much of our earlier discussion about the domain of constitutional justice would seem to have missed the point: The idea that constitutional concerns had to be immediate and nonnegotiable to be effective, for example, would be inapt if these concerns were meant to function only in the background of the Constitution.

But the connection between the domain of constitutional justice and the substance of our constitutional tradition is not like that. To be sure, our constitutional text and jurisprudence respond in part to concerns of political justice by architecting and protecting structural features of government—the horizontal separation of powers and the vertical distribution of authority within a federal structure. (James Madison was being neither disingenuous nor hopelessly naive when he initially favored governmental structure over the inclusion of a Bill of Rights in the nascent Constitution as the means of protecting liberty.) But we also have a liberty-bearing constitutional text and a relatively secure tradition of wide-bodied judicial interpretation of that text. Without undertaking an elaborate survey here, I think that the most active and secure ingredients of our liberty-bearing constitutional jurisprudence fit handsomely and recognizably with the broad concerns of equal membership on the one hand, and fair and open government on the other. The Supreme Court's preoccupation with racial and gender justice is clearly in service of its vision of equal membership, and so too, correctly understood, is much of the work of the modern Court in the area of religious liberty.[10] Many aspects of constitutional doctrine—ranging from the dominant themes of freedom of expression to the varied facets of voting rights and ballot access that have figured prominently in modern adjudication—reflect the Court's understanding of fair and open government.

An abiding concern with independence per se is somewhat less clearly manifest in our adjudicated constitutional tradition. In part, this is because our strong constitutional commitments to equal membership and fair and open government overlap with independence and obscure its discrete role in constitutional thought. In part, this is because aspects of independence lend themselves poorly to the categorical firmness of constitutional judgment. We have described independence as having a judgmental face (the opportunity of members of a political community to form judgments about their lives and the government under which they live their lives), and a behavioral face (the reasonable latitude of those members to lead the lives they choose). The judgmental face of independence is importantly protected by aspects of our jurisprudence of free expression, especially in those contexts where the stakes most clearly comprise the judgmental autonomy of the audience rather than the interests of the speaker or the political life of the community in any direct sense. More directly, there is a strong constitutional right of persons to believe what they choose to believe, sometimes assigned (misleadingly, in view of the precept's breadth) to the religion clauses. Less obviously, perhaps, our abiding reluctance to turn complete control of education over to the state is reflective of our commitment to judgmental independence.

To a greater degree than we realize, we depend upon the manifest restraint of legislative bodies in the United States for the maintenance of a broad sphere of independent conduct. Apart from a general avoidance of overreaching by legislatures—a strong reluctance, for example, to tell people what to wear, what to read, how to decorate their houses, with whom to associate in their homes, whom to hire for their personal guidance, and so on—there are specific legislative berths for discordant behavior that reflect a sensitivity to the concerns of independence: So-called "Mrs. Murphy" exemptions from antidiscrimination laws come to mind as an example. The Court, for its part, has policed untoward interference with behavioral independence in both acute and chronic circumstances. The acute cases involve intrusions that pass the ordinary and seem to be directing people in their intimate lives. The ability of seven justices in *Griswold v. Connecticut* to surmount the extreme and widely shared conceptual allergy to Lochnerizing[11] and strike down Connecticut's silly and pernicious law is an example of the Court in its acute independence mode. The chronic cases involve situations where there are more general structural grounds for judicial concern. Part of our tradition of religious liberty is an example: The sense shared by legislatures and courts that there is a core of religious activity—worship—that is beyond governmental interference in any but the most extreme of circumstances is best understood as a reflection of the distinct structure of organized religious practice, in which deeply personal matters are conducted in an open and public space.[12] Part of our tradition of free expression may also be best understood as a chronic concern with behavioral independence. When we consider our general reluctance to tolerate the suppression of the arts, we stand at the juncture of concerns with free and open government, judgmental independence, and behavioral independence.

In all, equal membership, fair and open government, and independence are robust and recognizable themes in our constitutional tradition. Further, our rather blunt and straightforward reading of the domain of constitutional justice which centers on these themes is superior on grounds of fit to most democratarian views of the domain of constitutional justice. As I intimated earlier, these views characteristically secure fit at some expense to either the foot or the shoe. Ely has trouble with the religion clauses, has to smuggle in a substantive commitment to equal membership by treating lapses from that standard as failures of rationality, and has nothing to offer to account for our durable post-*Griswold* tradition of a right to "privacy." Michelman in his democratarian phase argued for the rights of gays and lesbians on the ground that people who had realized their sexual identities were better voting citizens. Dworkin's view of democracy is sufficiently capacious to avoid these difficulties of fit, but his approach deflects attention to a controversial concept of democracy and makes these broad concerns dependent upon their connection to that view of democracy in a way that is both somewhat strained and unnecessary.[13]

The issue of fit is more problematic in the case of the opportunity to thrive and its more pointed entailment, the right to minimum welfare. Here, there is both a paucity of adjudicated constitutional outcomes that directly respond to material well-being, and good reason to conclude that the judiciary is institutionally unfit to be the primary protector of this dimension of constitutional justice. The question then becomes where one looks for fit. We have already seen a part of the answer: There are important threads of Supreme Court doctrine that seem awkward and anomalous on first encounter; they make good sense, however, when we posit the existence of the right to minimum welfare which is supported but not directly enforced by the constitutional judiciary.

But there is more to say about the question of fit in this connection. Were it the case that our polity regularly acted in a manner deeply and self-consciously inconsistent with the right to minimum welfare, there would be an objection on grounds of fit to the claim that this is an aspect of the domain of constitutional justice. Having concluded that primary responsibility for the maintenance of constitutional guarantees like the right to minimum welfare must lie with our popular political institutions, it is in important part to those institutions that we should look in considering the issue of fit. Despite our rather bad job of living up to our commitments in this regard, I think that there is evidence that we acknowledge the existence of a right to minimum welfare as a matter of political justice, the Constitution aside. These may seem somewhat hazardous times to make even modestly optimistic statements about the enduring commitments of our political community to the minimum welfare of its members. We are in the midst of "reforms" of social welfare programs that seem heartless and unjust in their consequences for some persons in our society—especially children and the disabled— and political sentiment appears coldly indifferent. But two things blunt the force of these contemporary political currents. First, as of this writing, our mean-spirited "reforms" of welfare legislation are still early experiments, and it is certainly to be hoped that true welfare reforms will be put in place to assure the opportunities of those willing to work hard on their own and their families behalf, and to protect the innocent young whose opportunities depend on a future that they may not otherwise come to enjoy at all. Second, if this hope is not realized, the burden of our discussion is that we will then be acting in stark contradiction to an important constitutional norm. A constitutional norm is not voided by passing misbehavior; it is violated.

These immediate times aside, we have at least aspired to secure the right to minimum welfare. There has been a pervasive social and political recognition of the need for a safety net, and efforts to implement a base of public support that satisfies the limited promise of that metaphor. Public or publicly supported education has not flourished in our time, but neither, emphatically, has it perished; we would, I strongly hope and believe, never retreat from our sustained commitment to a free basic education. Even in the face of our inability to rationalize the distribution of medical care, most if not all urban centers provide a network of public hospitals or some other mechanism by which the most urgent medical needs of the poor are met.

This focus on the pattern of popular political judgment raises the question of whether there is a negative question of fit lurking in our enduring economic arrangements, whether a view of the material dimension of constitutional justice that goes no further than the opportunity to lead a materially decent life is underinclusive of our actual constitutional commitments. The claim that this is so would invoke the durability of certain features of the economic landscape in the United States. We have, for example, consistently maintained a market economy. Does this suggest that our commitment to a market economy has constitutional dimensions, and in turn, that we have understated the material dimensions of the domain of constitutional justice? It does not, for this simple reason: Durable practices do not, without more, acquire constitutional tenure. However wise or foolhardy, the imposition of a flat tax would certainly be revolutionary; it would not be unconstitutional. We approached the point of asking whether our polity has acted in a manner that affronted the right to minimum welfare from the opposite direction. That is, we began with a freestanding argument in favor of recognizing the opportunity to a materially decent life as part of constitutional justice; then we observed that our constitutional jurisprudence on the best understanding not only was consistent with the recognition of the right to minimum welfare as an instantiation of that concern, but that important cases called for such an explanation. Then we asked, by way of a possible veto, in effect, whether our practices were deeply inconsistent with the existence of that right as a matter of constitutional justice.

I do not believe that we have the best of all possible constitutions, and emphatically I do not believe that we inhabit the best of all political worlds. I do, however, believe that we have a good Constitution, one that insists that we honor the fundamental demands of political justice. That we are denying many of our fellow citizens the opportunity to provide themselves and their families a materially decent life is a blight on our performance under the Constitution, not a reason to read justice out of the Constitution.

CHAPTER 9

The Birth Logic of
a Democratic Constitution

The Birth of the Constitution

T he birth of our Constitution was marked by two prominent and connected features. First, the process by which the Constitution was proposed and ratified differed radically from the means for constitutional change specified in the extant legal order that preceded the Constitution. At the national level, the Articles of Confederation announced themselves to be perpetual, and required for amendment the vote of the Continental Congress followed by confirmation in the state legislature of each of the compacting states. In contrast, Article VII of the Constitution provided for ratification by special state conventions, and required the ratification of only nine of the states to launch the Constitution as the highest law (binding only in the ratifying states, but fully destructive of the confederated regime nonetheless). At the state level, each of the thirteen state constitutions specified a procedure for amendment. Included were requirements that the state legislature initiate an amendment, that a supermajority of the electorate approve, and that the amendment take place after a certain year or in a specified cycle of years. Article VII's ratification procedure depended upon special state conventions rather than legislatures, contained no intra-state[1] supermajority requirement, and paid no homage to temporal requirements in the extant state constitutions. Thus, the Articles of Confederation were annulled and replaced, and the constitutions of the states were subordinated to a national government, all by a careful and elaborate process that ignored the specified channels for foundational change.[2]

Second, the process by which the Constitution was ratified was self-consciously democratic and driven—at least in part—by a common democratic mechanism, simple majority rule. Elections were held in each state for representatives who met in special conventions. While Article VII did not so specify, each of these conventions proceeded to make its ultimate decision by simple majority vote. In some states, the ratification vote was quite close; but simple majority will prevailed in these states and the Constitution was in fact launched.

This is largely familiar history,[3] which certainly deserves a place on the shelf of constitutional folklore. But does it deserve more? Does the birth of the Constitution offer important guidance for our contemporary understanding of constitutional choice and change? In particular, does this history suggest that the elaborate and intentionally burdensome requirements for amendment in Article V of the Constitution are no more secure than were the procedures for change specified in the Articles of Confederation or in the constitutions of the states prior to the launching of the Constitution?

Some commentators think so; they believe that the actual birth of the Constitution was consistent with and revealing of what we might call the birth logic of a democratic Constitution. They believe that an appropriately engaged, deliberative process culminating in an expression of majority will was sufficient to legitimate the dramatic revision of the foundations of government in the United States. Accordingly, they further believe, the enacted Constitution itself is subject to replacement or amendment by an appropriately engaged and deliberative process, whether or not that process conforms to the requirements of Article V.

This view of constitutional change is, to be sure, startling, but it is offered by those who hold it as a means of making our constitutional arrangements more rather than less congenial. We can see how this might be so. Suppose our understanding of the Constitution were deeply originalist, and driven by a particular view of the requirements of popular sovereignty. Pursuant to this understanding, the value and legitimacy of the Constitution would be crucially dependent on its embodying the expressed, detailed, and authoritative will of past constitutional majorities; and pursuant to this understanding, the essence of the job of interpreting the Constitution would lie in the recovery of that will. Were this our view, we would want constitutional adjudication to be fundamentally backward-looking, an exercise in what one commentator, Bruce Ackerman, has called "principled positivism."[4] If this were the best way to think of the Constitution, we should be skeptical about the narrow and arduous prescriptions for constitutional change offered by Article V. At best, they would offer only one possibility among many for the registration of the prevailing deliberative judgment of a political generation; at worst they would be an indefensible barrier to popular control of our constitutive arrangements.

Birth logic aside, the originalist account of our Constitution and our constitutionalism is wrong. As we have seen, the best, most compelling account of our constitutional institutions regards them as forward-looking and justice-seeking. The combination of popular constitutional decision-making through the ratification of constitutional text and judicial decision-making through the wide-bodied interpretation of that text is pragmatically well suited to the job of identifying the central features of political justice. The Constitution's text is fixed by popular constitutional decisions, and wisely, that text at its most critical points speaks at a high level of generality, inviting and requiring the active partnership of the constitutional judiciary in the enterprise of shaping the contours of constitutional justice.

In turn, I believe that the Article V requirements for the amendment of the Constitution are an attractive part of the pragmatic, justice-seeking quality of our constitutional institutions. By design, they make the Constitution hard to amend, and by design, they require not just large majorities, but a broad geographic consensus. The obduracy of the Constitution to amendment requires of members of the ratifying generation that they choose for the Constitution principles and provisions not just for themselves but for their children and their children's children; while the geographic diversity demanded by Article V is a reasonable proxy for a broad diversity of circumstance among those who must join in endorsing changes in the text of the Constitution. The result is a structural tendency towards the popular choice of general principles attractive and acceptable to persons in a variety of actual human circumstance, imagining their application over time to generations unborn in circumstances unknown.

So we have what seems a mismatch: an otherwise compelling account of our constitutional institutions that favors a pragmatic, justice-seeking Constitution, with a proactive constitutional judiciary in partnership with a popular, constitutional amendment process shaped by Article V; but a birth logic which, it is claimed, favors instead a backward-looking constitutional judiciary and an amendment process ultimately requiring only the determined will of deliberative majorities.

In this chapter, I hope to dispel this illusion of mismatch by offering a different, and, I believe, better understanding of the birth logic of a democratic constitution. The stakes here overreach our own national circumstance: If determined majorities are free to overturn the constitutive arrangements which restrain their considered will, then all democratic constitutional arrangements are more fragile than is commonly supposed.

Birth Lessons

We need at the outset to understand what sort of guidance we can and cannot plausibly expect from the birthing of the Constitution. In particular, we need to set aside the clearly false idea that there is a necessary symmetry between the conditions under which a regime of government is born and those under which it can be changed or replaced, that the "sovereign" which birthed a constitution is thereby entitled to revoke or remake its work, or that the precedent of a constitution's birth stipulates the conditions of its demise.

There is no logical or necessary connection between the formal provenance of a constitution, its legitimacy, and the circumstances under which it can be revoked and changed. Imagine a country ruled by generations of despotic monarchs until the moment that Queen Liza assumes the crown. Liza is a democrat through and through, and she commissions the leading thinkers of her land to fashion a democratic constitution, which constitution she then imposes by decree upon her people. The people respond by participating in the decreed elections; the congress is formed, and the president elected; and the government is launched. If it is a well-formed democratic government, and the population salutes, it is legitimate by democratic lights. Once democracy thus takes hold, Liza has an assured place among her nation's heroes, but she does not have ongoing sovereign authority to revoke or amend the constitution. Were Liza to suffer a change of heart, and wax nostalgic for the days of the monarchy, the democratic government to which she gave birth would (we imagine), and certainly should treat her impulse as an unfortunate, undemocratic, and unconstitutional attempt to usurp the authority of the people, their elected representatives, and the constitution itself. A democratic constitution can name and create the popular sovereign; it can render obsolete and even repugnant its own nondemocratic parent.

So too, an imperfect democratic order can irreversibly work itself fine, and a significantly flawed democratic process can launch a constitutional order which from the first or eventually overcomes its flaws. We need no imagined or exotic example of this proposition at work: Our own constitutional ratification process, though wonderfully democratic by the standards of its time, involved an exclusive electorate of white, propertied males. It would be preposterous to suggest that the exclusionary features that marked the group that gave birth (à la Zeus) to the Constitution also confer on contemporary white, propertied males the power to alter or abolish our constitutional order by a preponderance of judgment—however thoughtful it might be—among themselves.

To make sense of arguments about the birth logic of the Constitution, accordingly, we have to understand them as claiming something other than a natural symmetry or normative identity between the circumstances that launched the Constitution and those that would legitimate contemporary attempts to change the Constitution. We must understand claims about the birth logic of the Constitution as arguing for something less strong and direct than that.

Two possibilities suggest themselves on behalf of those who argue that the machinery for amendment specified in Article V of the Constitution is not exclusive. The first is a normative claim about political justice: It holds that a democratic people have the endemic authority to remake their constitutive arrangements at will; and it uses the Founding as example rather than binding authority. The second is an interpretive claim: It holds that Article V is best read as offering suggestions about the process for amending the Constitution, not as stipulating an exclusive protocol for so doing; and it uses the Founding as evidence of the framers' state of mind. The normative claim argues that the framers were in general wise and in this instance they were indeed right—right to ignore extant constraints and to submit the draft Constitution to an ad hoc, democratically composed process. The interpretive claim argues that—whether or not they were actually right in believing themselves to have the license to ignore extant constitutive law—the framers must have meant for succeeding generations to have the same license to amend their constitutive arrangements that they took themselves to have, and that Article V should be read to reflect their intention in this regard.

It is the normative argument which must do the lion's share of the work for the Article V revisionists. The text of Article V—in isolation and in the context of the Constitution as a whole—is far from congenial to their position. The same is true of our constitutional practice over time, which has consistently named Article V as the exclusive source of popular amendment of the Constitution.[5] This is not to say that imaginative interpretive efforts to find room for extra–Article V amendment of the Constitution are doomed to failure, but rather, that the possibility of their success is crucially dependent upon our being persuaded that an important principle of political justice is vindicated by this strained reading of text and history. Even the somewhat doubtful venture of reading our constitutional text and practice through the lens of the framers' rhetoric and behavior in the face of their fight for national survival ultimately depends on a prior normative judgment: The license to disregard extant legal constraints towards which the words and the acts of the founding generation gestured can be read broadly as the license of all democratic peoples at all times, or much more narrowly, as the license of a democratic people under the exceptional circumstances of constitutional breakdown. The choice between these readings can only be justified by the shape of the normative understanding brought to the table by the interpreter. Thus, the normative argument for disregarding Article V has first claim on our attention.

The normative argument from the Founding does not make the mistake of equating the conditions of a regime's birth with the preconditions of legitimate change of that regime. Read in this way, birth logic claims can be rescued from plain error. But this merely gets us to the point of interesting disagreement. So read, after all, these claims still take from the example of the founding of our Constitution the lesson that in a democracy a constitution is freely amendable by an appropriately deliberative democratic process, notwithstanding express provisions—like Article V in our own Constitution—which offer narrow and rather burdensome requirements for any amendment.

Some would take the normative lesson of the Constitution's birth still further, and argue that simple majority rule is an appropriate metric of consensus for constitutional change. Here, of course, the example of the Founding itself, even if read for all that it could be worth, is less helpful to Article V revisionists. Article VII's requirements for ratification are roughly congruent with the heart of Article V's requirements for amendment: Where the agreement of nine-thirteenths of the states was necessary to launch the Constitution, the agreement of three-quarters is required for its amendment; in both cases the Constitution is silent on the question of what metric of consensus within each state is appropriate, and simple majority rule has been the uniform norm in lieu of a more demanding constitutional stipulation.

But even if the example of the Founding falls considerably short of endorsing majority rule, it is the disparity between majority rule and the requirements of Article V that lies at the heart of the normative claim. In the end, the argument is a simple one: The fact that reflective political majorities cannot effectuate constitutional change is an embarrassment to the democratic foundations of our constitutionalism. I hope to demonstrate that this argument is false.

Amendment and Change

There is one other preliminary matter that will clarify our discussion. No one denies that judicial understandings of the Constitution have changed—sometimes rather sharply and dramatically—over time, and that many of these changes in understanding have occurred without formal, Article V amendment of the text of the Constitution. The most prominent of these alterations of judicial course is the "switch in time"—those few months in 1937 in the space of which the Supreme Court effectively repudiated the substantive due process tradition of which *Lochner v. New York* has become the reviled symbol, and reshaped the prevailing jurisprudence of the Commerce Clause—in the course of which the Court stepped aside and permitted Congress to pursue its New Deal agenda. If each relatively dramatic and apparently enduring change in constitutional doctrine counted as an "amendment" of the Constitution, then obviously Article V could not be regarded as the exclusive means of amending the Constitution.

But the challenge to the exclusivity of Article V is meant to have more bite than that. We can better understand the source of that bite if we think about the prospect of a change in constitutional understanding from the standpoint of a judge. Imagine that it is 1937, and all that actually happened has happened. A justice of the Supreme Court, heretofore a champion of a rather restrictive view of the Commerce Clause, sits in his study, and decides that, notwithstanding his prior judgment, Congress should have broad, largely unfettered authority to pursue its New Deal agenda. Now we can imagine two very different sorts of reasons our justice might have for this conversion. Having been educated by experience of and reflection upon the Great Depression and its aftermath, he might have altered his judgment as to the best understanding of the Constitution in the time and place he found the nation and its economy. Or, looking back over the political events of the last months or years, he might believe that an appropriately formed and expressed political consensus had emerged and produced a popular amendment to the Constitution, just as though the text had been formally amended in accord with Article V. In the first story, the Constitution has remained constant but the judge's understanding of it has changed; we can call this the *judgmental* account. In the second, the Constitution itself has changed, and this is the reason that the judge has altered his understanding of what it permits; we can call this the *positivist* account.

Now it is important to note that both the judgmental and the positivist account can and are likely to be sensitive to history and social context. Both might even be sensitive to the same features of the practical world on occasion. For example, both the judgmental and the positivist account might focus on an increasingly broad and sustained view among the members of our political community that the Commerce Clause was being improperly invoked by the Supreme Court to impede the national recovery effort; for the justice in the judgmental account, this mounting consensus might be an important reason to reconsider his views. But the difference between these accounts is profound, and profoundly important. In the judgmental account, it is the judge's own judgment that governs her interpretive obligation; in the positivist account, it is the formation of a popular consensus under stipulated extra–Article V circumstances that governs her interpretive obligation.

Article V revisionists are committed to some form of the positivist account of non–Article V constitutional change. They believe that an appropriately formed non–Article V consensus changes the

Constitution, and binds conscientious judges and all other constitutional actors to accordingly. This is what makes their view worth arguing about.

Choosing Voting Rules in Thin Air

Imagine that, in a faculty meeting, a motion is made to conduct a particular vote by secret ballot. This is an irregular and controversial proposal, and the inevitable question arises: How is the secondary, procedural vote—the vote, that is, on how the principal vote is to be conducted—itself to be conducted? Questions of this sort are latent in any vote about how to vote; within a regime of rules they are typically resolved by reference to rules—explicit or implied, specific or default—about changing the rules. But when a choice of this sort must be made outside any existing system of rules, when the root governing rules are themselves being chosen, matters become conundral.

This is what makes the question of how a democratic constitution gets started so interesting. A theocratic community has a great conceptual advantage: A vision is seen, a heavenly voice heard, or a sacred tablet unearthed; by one means or another the divine force announces its presence and dictates ground rules for the holy. But in a community committed to self-rule, the constitutional details of democratic government must be chosen by a process that is itself at least roughly democratic. In such a setting the problem of what preconstitutional rules should be followed for choosing the constitutional rules for postconstitutional political choices has real bite. Actually, the problem starts somewhat further back, at the stage of the constitutional convention.

Suppose that we are in the remarkable position of forming a new government, unencumbered by our legal past. (We needn't fill in the hypothetical details, but we can imagine a constitutional convention held after revolution has deposed an unpopular monarch, or on the occasion of a group of persons gathered to form an ongoing society on virgin territory, with no lingering allegiances to or fondness for the governmental arrangements in our states of origin.) And suppose that we are elected delegates,[6] charged with the job of drafting a constitution and submitting it to our fellow citizens for ratification. Among us, there is broad agreement that the government must be democratic, and a shared, general picture of what qualifies a government as democratic; but, of course, there are important details about which there is not wide agreement.

Our first question will be how to resolve our substantive disagreements at the convention stage, where we are fashioning a draft constitution to propose to the broader population for ratification. Various internal procedural issues will arise which—as social choice theory reminds us—may have important consequences. Among these is the question of what voting rule we should follow in making our substantive decisions. Imagine that three protocols emerge as rivals: simple majority rule, supermajority rule (pegged at two-thirds of those voting), and unanimity.

The question is this: By what voting protocol will we make the election between the rival protocols (and, probably, make our other decisions about procedures at the convention as well)? We might well choose simple majority rule. The reflex in democratic assemblies to act on simple majority rule is so entrenched and common that we might not even recognize that we have any other possibility. But even if we were reflective about this first question, the choice of simple majority rule at this default stage is supported by pragmatic, epistemic, and equitable concerns. First, simple majority rule will almost certainly produce answers to these initial procedural questions, as opposed to locking us in possible stalemate. Second, as we make various procedural choices in order to get our convention going, there is no apparent reason to adopt a rule that deflects close choices towards the status quo, no policy or epistemic reason for preferring inaction to action supported by a majority of those who attend. And third, simple majority rule has the equitable virtue of counting each voter as one and giving each one equal weight; any supermajority rule confers on those who favor the status quo a minority veto over change. (We see this most vividly in a regime of unanimity, which confers on any one resister the authority to veto colleagues.)

But this hypothesized selection of simple majority as the mechanism for choosing, inter alia, among voting rules at this stage in our proceedings must not be read for more than it is worth. On a comparatively superficial level, there is this obvious but nagging question: Who were the "we" that chose simple majority rule, and by what voting rule did "we" act? Presumably, we were the totality of the delegates, representing in turn the totality of the parties who are recognized as members or putative members of the forthcoming polity; and presumably, in some sense or another—informally perhaps or by implication—we all gave our consent to the choice of simple majority rule for the purpose of our first official decisions. We did so by showing up and participating, at least, and possibly by more explicit means as well.

Lurking behind this observation is the deeper sense that, in principle, the constitution—and before the constitution, the constitutive process by which the constitution is drawn—ought to be acceptable to every member or group within the polity-to-be. Theoretical unanimity is the basal condition of political legitimacy. Gathering together to form our community we agree to be bound by a process which we hope will eventually lead to the adoption of a constitution, and as the first step, we adopt what seems a fair and effective voting process, a natural process, to get us started, namely, simple majority rule. But behind even this first step is the requirement of consent to go forward; and in front of this step is the reasonable prospect that decisions taken by a majority of those assembled, taken as a whole, ought to be acceptable to each member of the political community. As against this basal aspiration of the constitutional project, the intra-assembly equitable virtues of majority rule must be seen as comparatively superficial and contextual.

Back in our constitutional convention we next confront the question of which voting rule—simple majority, supermajority, or unanimity—we will pursue in resolving the substantive questions that are bound to divide us as we go about the business of drafting a constitution. Much the same general concerns confront us as we vote—by simple majority rule—on this question, but the picture has changed somewhat. Initially, we were choosing a pump-priming mechanism to get us started; we were, in effect, constituting the "we" that would deliberate about the new constitution. Now we are in a position to think as a group about what ongoing mechanism will best suit our enterprise of drafting a constitution. We may have reason to resist the rush to simple majority rule. The two-thirds majority or unanimity rules would encourage reflection and deliberation, and press towards compromise and consensus, towards constitutional arrangements that can enjoy the support of a broad range of the group that will live under the constitution; they would do so, however, at the risk of delay, possibly even the collapse of our constitutional convention in stalemate. Equitable concerns among ourselves as delegates continue to favor simple majority rule, but they are comparatively superficial; deeper is the concern that our process lead to a constitution that in principle can be acceptable to all the members of the new political community.

For all of this, given the urgency in getting the job of constitution-making done and the process of governance underway, simple majority rule may well be the preferred alternative, but that is not what is important when we step back from our hypothetical world to our inquiry into the birth logic of a democratic constitution. What is important is this: First, our choice of simple majority rule to make our choices about procedure at our constitutional convention did not foreclose the possibility that we would choose the two-thirds rule as the protocol for our subsequent choices about the constitution itself; and second, neither of these choices turned upon some deep and essential truth about fair democratic processes. Simple majority rule, at its strongest, sponsors a fair and reasonable process, one that ought to commend itself to the representatives of a free and democratic people under some circumstances.

It bears emphasis that the point is not that having adopted simple majority rule as our initial mechanism of choice we have thereby legitimated any set of mechanisms that we choose to put in place. The democratic provenance of governing arrangements does not certify those arrangements. A hereditary monarchy chosen by a perfectly composed democratic process is neither democratic nor just. Rather, the point is stronger and perhaps more provocative: The pragmatic, epistemic, and normative features of voting rules need to be evaluated in context and while democracy is a necessary feature of just and sensible arrangements for governance, simple majority rule is not.

Constituting "The People"

We are not through, of course, with either our constitution-drafting fiction or our birth logic analysis; in fact, we've barely begun. Most of our work at the convention stage will concern the substantive provisions of our constitution. In the most general of terms, these provisions will have at least two features of interest: First, they will parse between those matters that are decided in the constitution itself and those that are directed to the ordinary, ongoing political process of our nascent state; second, they will put in place the machinery of ordinary politics. For our purposes here, we will assume that the substance of the constitution is much like the substance of our actual Constitution, that relatively few matters are concluded in the constitution itself, and that the machinery of ordinary politics is more or less appropriately democratic. We'll consider the importance of these assumptions a little further on.

In our role as drafters of the constitution, we will also need to set the terms by which the constitution will be ratified, the kind of approval our draft will have to receive from the population of our political community before it becomes—by its own, formal terms— valid and binding. (I add the qualifying phrase because no document and accompanying process can literally command its own authority; Hans Kelsen's *Grundnorm* or H. L. A. Hart's "ultimate rule of recognition" are constructs that reflect the conceptual shape of a regime of rules that has come to enjoy and continues to enjoy social acceptance.) We also need to set the terms by which the constitution can subsequently be amended. By now you will have anticipated the direction in which I hope to extend the argument: As with the two choices of voting rules we made at the convention stage, these two choices at the constitution stage need not be the same; and as with our earlier choices, these choices are not rigidly preordained by fundamental requirements of democracy or justice. More pointedly and clearly, the choice of simple majority rule is not insisted upon by either democracy or justice.

Let us begin with ratification. Suppose for a moment that our proposed government is rather small in scale; imagine, for example, that we are all independent settlers who have carved up a small island geographically into our respective parcels, the boundaries of which we more or less regularly respect as a modus vivendi; our proposed constitution is intended to replace this temporary arrangement with the machinery for systematic governance. We might well take the view that only those of us who support the constitution should be bound by it—that simple majority rule was fine for drafting, but that in the end the root formation of a political community requires actual consent. This would lead us to a voting rule requiring unanimous support among those who will become part of our new constitutional community, and probably, the support of a large percentage of the island population before the constitution becomes effective at all.

Or, in contrast, we might think that a simple majority vote is the best mechanism for ratification, on the same sorts of grounds that have attracted us to that rule in our earlier discussion. Here, majority rule is no more decisive than any other rule, but it does make acceptance of the constitution more likely. The same back-and-forth epistemic arguments can be made, and the limited form of fairness offered by majority rule remains in place, though offset rather directly and powerfully by the claim that actual consent is requisite to inclusion in a new political community.

Or, yet again, we might believe that while the consent of each new member is not required to form our political community, a supermajority requirement nevertheless is appropriate: to the general advantages of reflection and deliberation of a supermajority process, there would be added the practical and normative virtues of broad consensus as the predicate for the formation of a new political community. The normative virtues of broad consensus should be obvious: Consensus points in the direction of theoretical unanimity.

Now things are getting problematic for our constitution-drafting enterprise. Here there are serious and conflicting contenders for what might seem to be the most crucial voting event of all, the ratification or rejection of our proposed constitution. There is no obvious rule offered by the concept of democracy from which deviation must be justified, but rather various views of how a new political community is appropriately launched. Ironically, the judgment between these views isn't going to be made directly by the members of the political community at all, but rather by us, delegates of the community. We are either voting by simple or supermajority rule, and none of us, presumably, think that our consensus should actually serve to ratify the draft constitution. Yet we are going to have to make the election between these ratification rules for the community as a whole, using only the general voting rule we have chosen to operate with in convention.

Even if we were to pass the choice of the appropriate ratifying protocol on to the community as a whole as an open question, we could not really avoid the conundral aspects of the situation. What voting mechanism should the community as a whole use for making this choice between ratifying protocols? Suppose, for example, the community as a whole voted by simple majority vote that the ratification protocol should itself be simple majority vote—that alone could not satisfy those committed to another voting protocol that they were wrong.

If our proposed constitutional community were larger in scale than our island community, and already divided into groups that enjoyed geographic contiguity and cultural affinity, we might think that what best suited the ratification vote was a procedure that elicited the consent of these extant groups, rather than the consent of each individual. The actual ratification requirements of the United States Constitution had some of this flavor, but in an interestingly mixed form. Only those states that ratified the Constitution would be bound by it as members of the United States, and further, the Constitution would become effective only if ratified by nine of the thirteen states. What is curious about the ratification protocol of Article VII is that while it depends heavily on the extant states as the relevant units of consent, it is at considerable pains to avoid the existing machinery of governance in those states, calling for ratification by special state constitutional conventions rather than by the state legislatures. Hence a hybrid process emerged in which simple majorities would ultimately determine state ratification outcomes but only those states that consented would be bound, and a supermajority of states (three-quarters, rounded down) would have to consent for the Constitution to be operative at all. This is far different than a mere simple majority requirement, and much more like the state supermajority requirements of the Article V amendment process than birth logic–simple majority rule theorists commonly recognize.

And what of the amendment procedure for our new community constitution? As I suggested early on—in connection with our actual Constitution—we have a good reason for wanting the constitution to be obdurate to change. If popular constitutional decision-making proceeds on the assumption that constitutional provisions will endure for a very long time, salutary tendencies will be encouraged: The range of circumstance over one's own life, the life of one's children, and their children in turn, encourages a generality of perspective that draws away from self-interest and towards the choice of reasonable ground rules for all; and the need to fashion the liberty-bearing provisions of the Constitution in ignorance of many of the details of social life to which they will come to be applied in the future encourages a generality of description that invites and requires the partnership of a constitutional judiciary, and discourages attempts by the founding generation to overconstitutionalize political choice. If it is understood from the outset that the constitution will be obdurate to change, these effects of well-formed rules for amendment kick in long before the first effort to amend the constitution; the anticipation of the durability of the constitution will impact not just on the decision whether to ratify the proposed constitution, but on the constitutional convention itself. If, as we have reason to hope, an obdurate constitution will in this fashion inspire careful, general, long-range reflection, then we can regard it as a virtue, not a liability, that in its domain the constitution resists the passions of the moment.

There is, of course, an additional, less savory, incentive (we won't call it a reason) that we as the founding generation have for making our constitution hard to amend. We may have a natural desire to resolve the questions of constitutional structure not just for ourselves but for posterity. We trust ourselves, perhaps, but not those who will succeed us in stewardship of our political community. This is not a particularly attractive picture, perhaps; but both the appeal and the liability of this generational chauvinism, it should be observed, are much blunted by the very act of making our constitution obdurate to change. We, the founding generation, have to live with this constitution for many years ourselves, and after us, our progeny; precisely because our constitution is obdurate to change, we are constrained to broad issues of structure and general propositions of political justice. In effect, by electing to extend our influence over time, we are required to reduce its substantive scope.

As with ratification, if our constitutional community is reasonably large, procedures for amendment may take account of groups—like states, of course—that enjoy geographic contiguity and cultural affinity. This might be so on either of two conceptually distinct grounds. We might hold the view that these groups have so much in common that they reflect the relevant units of agreement; we might hold, that is, that these groups are themselves the entities that are entitled to have a say—a vote or veto—about constitutive arrangements. Even if we did not believe that, we might well believe that by insisting on agreement among such groups we introduce a diversity of value and circumstance—a diversity, in sum, of perspective—that makes for judgments better suited to the project of doing justice among a diverse people, considered from the perspective of the present population and future populations who presumptively will be living under the same or similar constitutional arrangements. In the latter case we would make group votes the measure of constitutive agreement, even though it was individuals rather than groups who were the pertinent units.

Now all this speculation about the voting procedures we might deploy at various stages in the process of constitution-making is meant to be in aid of four propositions. First, there are various voting protocols that a political community deeply committed in principle to democracy and democratic procedures might choose. Second, a democratic community might quite sensibly choose different procedures for different purposes, and hence for different stages in the process of establishing and maintaining a written constitution. Third, the conundrum of what voting protocol a group should employ in order to decide what voting protocol it should employ becomes a serious matter at critical intervals like the ratification of a constitution. And fourth, ratification and amendment protocols more or less like those specified in Article VII and Article V of the Constitution make reasonably good sense for a constitutional regime committed to the project of seeking political justice. I mean for present purposes to be modest about this last point: I do not claim that a political community that aspires to justice requires a constitution that is obdurate to change, or that it requires a written constitution at all; nor do I claim that a polity with a written, enduring constitution is necessarily superior to one that lacks such an amenity. What I do mean to claim is that an enduring constitution is a sensible institutional design for the ongoing pursuit of political justice in a political community, and that an amendment procedure roughly like that in Article V is a sensible way, inter alia, of making the Constitution an enduring one.

Changing the Rules?

Now let us suppose that we have passed through both the convention and ratification stages. We have in place a constitution; for convenience, we'll imagine that its provisions are very close to those actually chosen in the United States Constitution. Not only has our constitution been formally ratified, it has taken hold firmly as a matter of social practice. Our constitution has provisions that permit amendment, but only under circumstances considerably more arduous than formal deliberation followed by simple majority support for change (its provisions are more or less like those of our actual Article V). At the convention stage we framers proposed these amendment procedures and at the ratification stage the members of our political community accepted our proposal. Whatever choice among the competing voting mechanisms was made, it is fair to say that the provisions for amendment were a reasoned choice, in service of democratic justice. They were perceived as making more likely that the collaboration of popular and judicial constitutional decision-making for which the new constitution provided would produce good results.

After a time, a movement for constitutional change takes form in our political community. The proposed change appears to enjoy substantial popular support, but to the frustration of those who favor the change, it appears that the attempt to comply with the constitution's requirements for amendment will fail. Accordingly, the leaders of the movement for change call on the legislature, by simple majority vote, to convene a special national convention of elected representatives, who after a careful deliberative process, will in turn vote by simple majority to approve or disapprove the proposed change. (Or perhaps they ask the legislature to authorize a process in which a national referendum figures prominently. What is important is that they ask for a process other than those authorized in the amendment provisions of our constitution.) Now the question arises: Must our constitution's stipulation of the requirements for amendment be followed, or can an alternative deliberative process, ultimately keyed to a simple majority vote, be substituted?

We should take a moment to be clear about what we are asking. The question is not how history in our community might actually go: whether the legislature is likely to call a special national convention or institute a national referendum, whether an amendment would be approved, whether the courts would endorse an amendment created outside the terms of the constitution, or how the population at large would respond to this event. Rather, the question is how conscientious political actors should act: whether the leaders would be right to call on the legislature to act in this unusual way, whether the legislature should consider itself free to agree, whether the courts should respect an amendment created in this way, and whether we as citizens should celebrate or protest this enlargement of the amending power.

This is a good moment to leave behind our hypothetical world with its hypothetical constitution and turn to our world, with our Constitution, complete with Article V as it actually is. The question we arrived at in our hypothetical world is precisely the question upon which the validity of the normative claim advanced by the Article V revisionists turns.

Article V and "The People"

What can be said in support of the idea that the amending procedures of Article V can be freely circumvented? We can begin with a particular understanding of popular sovereignty in a democratic state: The government belongs to the people; it was created by them and it owes its legitimacy to their initial and ongoing acceptance. The people cannot bind themselves to a constitution entrenched against their decision to amend it. If they could do this, they could bind themselves to the rule of a hereditary monarchy. Accordingly, when, after careful deliberation, a majority of the people are settled in the view that their government should be changed, it should be changed. The democratic provenance of a constitutional regime is not enough to make it democratic. There must be ongoing power vested in the people; and the majority of the people must enjoy the power to remake their government when the need arises. That is the lesson of the founding of the Constitution. On this account, it follows that the people can always change their government by simple deliberative majority action.

There is an important truth in this argument. In a democracy government does indeed belong to the people, and that proposition is more fundamental than the mechanical framework of government through which the democratic ideal is sought to be realized at any given time or place. Furthermore, there are surely constitutional arrangements that could be arrived at in a democratically laudable process that would be unacceptable from the vantage of political justice, precisely because of their undemocratic substance.

But to invoke "the people" is to invoke what is at best a metaphor, and here, as is often the case in constitutional discourse, that metaphor obscures rather than reveals many important questions. Modern democracies consist of persons who to some, quite possibly substantial, degree share a cultural and political identity, to be sure, but among those persons are groups and individuals who differ in significant ways over serious matters. Every protocol for revealing the state of popular judgment or preference—including elaborate measures of electoral outcomes over a period of time—offers at best one possible depiction of the sensibilities of "the people" as a whole.

For the moment, let us set aside the obvious problem of how a particular arithmetic division among the national population should be resolved into a choice among competing options, and assume that we are concerned only with the full picture, with a complete report of the divergent votes. Even such a complete report, taken on its own terms, is at best only one possible representation of "the people." How many people actually voted? What were the choices offered them? How were issues joined or severed, and how were they functionally ordered? What information and arguments were available? Was debate free and extensive? Did the circumstances of the vote conduce to reflection or reflexion? And on and on: We know enough about human nature, group choice, and the complexities of political events more generally to recognize that no encompassable electoral event or sequence of events can give us the ineffable substance of "the people," even if we have in mind the actual persons who are alive and citizens of our polity within a relatively narrow period of time.

When we take up the problem we laid aside a moment ago, the point deepens. Competing mechanisms for converting division into choice are just that. Even ignoring the nonarithmetic difficulties of the previous paragraph, when have "the people" spoken? When 51 percent of the voting population express a uniform choice? 66 percent? 75 percent? Or—to introduce some of the problems of our actual constitutional world—if simple majorities in three-quarters of the states support option X but that option falls slightly short of majority support in the nation as a whole, where a small overall majority favor option Y: Does option X or option Y better represent "the people"? This is why we had hard choices among voting protocols to make at every step along the way in the launching of our constitution in the first place.

The point of all this is not that there are no reasons sounding in the values of democracy for preferring one protocol of political choice over another, but rather that the choice of protocols must be defended, and further that the defense of a given protocol must be seen in the context of a rather thick understanding of the circumstances in which it is meant to operate. We never have "the people" in a very interesting or durable sense; what we have are various mechanisms for doing the best we can to get reports or representations of "the people." More accurately, we have various mechanisms for treating the competing and shifting judgments and preferences of the members of a political community fairly, and for doing justice among those members.

Within these competing mechanisms, simple majority rule has no a priori claim to pride of place. Simple arithmetic intuition cannot do the work being asked of it by those who want to treat democracy, rule by the people, and simple majority rule as synonymous. Imagine our reaction if one of our friends returned from a tennis match and announced that the player who was treated by all the other spectators and the officials as having lost had in fact played much the better game, and further, that the scoring of tennis was poorly calculated to award the win to the better player. Our friend's rationale for this pair of propositions is simply this: Given the game-set-match scoring protocol of a tennis match, it is entirely possible that the person who wins the most points can lose the game. Now our friend might prove in the end to be right, of course. But even in a matter as simple as tennis, the question of whether the game would be better or worse if the person with the most single points won—even the narrower question of whether the game would then be a better measure of the ability of contending players—is surely complex enough to require more than the blind invocation of arithmetic. When we are considering the elaborate institutional arrangements that compose an ongoing democratic government and the array of concerns that go into an evaluation of those arrangements, the superficial appeal of simple arithmetic is far more misleading.

It is possible, of course, that upon reflection we would conclude that tennis would be a better game if played on a simple highest-number-of-points basis; and likewise, possible that we would come to think that some mechanism centering on simple majority rule would be the most democratic—or the most just, or both—way of connecting the members of a political community with the ultimate destiny of their community. But either of these judgments needs support from an argument that puts the protocol it champions in contest with other possible or suggested protocols and defends it as superior. An appeal to "the people" is only interesting as a rhetorical way of presenting the result of such a contest; it does not take us behind or above the contest.

The claim that Article V can be displaced spontaneously by a less onerous procedure for amendment, accordingly, must depend on more than simple arithmetic. What is required is support for the proposition that—considering the overall structure of governance contemplated by the Constitution—it is anathema to democracy for "the people" to be separated from the substance of their Constitution by the rigors of Article V.

The question of Article V's compatibility with democracy is critical in turn to the question of whether our constitutional practice as a whole is democratic. That question, which is our focus in Chapter 10, depends in part on our evaluation of Article V. It will by now come as no surprise to the reader that I use the occasion of that discussion to rise to the defense of Article V. For the moment, however, I want to consider what a democratic people can do when their constitution is *not* appropriately connected to popular judgment.

A Democratically Deficient Constitution— Responding to Breakdown

Suppose we return to our hypothetical constitutional world and stipulate that our constitution is inappropriately resistant to change. Even so, how could the claim that this is true become an argument for circumventing the amendment requirements of our constitution? Why isn't this simply an argument for amending the amendment provisions? After all, our constitution is law, and it specifies exclusive procedures for its own amendment. And we arrived at our constitutional arrangements, including the procedures for amending the constitution, in the course of an elaborate and careful series of events, events aimed at securing sound results themselves fairly arrived at from the perspective of constitutional democracy.

To have grounds for circumventing the constitutionally stipulated requirements for amendment, the leaders of the movement for constitutional change in our hypothetical political community must insist that their objection is deeper than a mere disagreement about whether a rival mechanism is a better amendment procedure. Their claim must be that the constitution as it stands is in some important sense inconsistent with the sound governance of the community, that the amendment procedures specified in the constitution are a more or less decisive barrier to constitutional change, and are an inappropriate means for a democratic community to make constitutional choices, and further, that these procedures are functionally self-entrenching, that the same qualities which make them undemocratic serve as a practical matter to immunize them from change.

If the complaint of those who want to circumvent the constitutionally specified procedure for amendment does not satisfy these conditions of entrenched infirmity, then they face the problem we've already hinted at, of having no democratic grounds upon which they can rely. They argue that we as a political community would be better off if our protocol for constitutional amendment were different; others strongly disagree. The matter, all agree, should be referred to the people, and the constitution stipulates the representation of the people that should govern constitutional choices. If those who would disregard that representation claim only that it could be improved upon, they have not given us a reason to disregard it, only a reason to change it in conformity with its requirements. This isn't a matter for the courts or the legislature, but rather for the people, acting in accord with the constitution's amendment procedures.

So we have made some headway. We have sketched, in effect, the circumstances of constitutional breakdown, and determined that these are the conditions of a license for a democratic polity to ignore its own constitution's requirements for constitutional change: (a) aspects of the constitutional regime are critically deficient, in that they are an obstacle to sound governance at a moment of considerable need; (b) the specified amendment procedures make amendment of the regime impossible or extremely unlikely, inducing a kind of paralysis; and (c) the specified amendment procedures are in some deep sense a failed representation of the people.

By now, you may have anticipated the regressive nature of the problem. Suppose that the leaders of the movement for constitutional change in our hypothetical community argue that what we have said must be true in order to justify a departure from the constitution's specified means for amendment is indeed true. They argue that the amendment provisions of the constitution are both radically infirm and entrenched by virtue of that infirmity. Not everyone agrees that either or both of the propositions are true, we may assume. Who is to decide?

This is like our earlier problem of how to choose the mechanism for ratifying the constitution, but with a particular bite: We find ourselves in the unhappy position of having to decide a prickly question of democratic choice in order to select the mechanism for deciding a prickly question of democratic choice. How ought we to proceed?

It might seem that the circumstances dictate the choice of decision-maker. In our story, the leaders of the movement for constitutional change turn first to the legislature for authorization of their proposed unorthodox amendment process. Should the legislature grant their request and launch such a process, citizens will surely be involved—informally as a matter of debate, and formally, when something or someone is put to the vote. And if anything purporting to be a constitutional amendment ultimately emerges from the renegade process, the high court will almost certainly be called upon to pass on its validity. Aren't each of these groups— legislature, citizens, high court—nominated by circumstance as the constitutional decision-maker in their time and place?

Matters are not quite that simple, of course. Each of these groups may indeed become the decision-maker, in a sense, but as to any of these groups it might be the case that the appropriate course involves firm deference to another group or process. Here there is good reason for deference to the people, since popular control of some sort is the abiding commitment of the amendment requirements in our hypothetical constitution, just as in Article V in the actual Constitution. But the constitution's representation of the people for purposes of amendment is being challenged as deeply infirm and impossibly entrenched. What can replace that representation as the appropriate representation of the people?

Perhaps we can do no better than to offer this prescription: No political actor—member of congress, justice of the supreme court, or conscientious citizen—should lightly or independently reach the conclusion that the circumstances of constitutional breakdown obtain. To our three conditions of constitutional breakdown we must add a requirement of obviousness and consensus: Only when there is widespread agreement that these three conditions obtain should any political actor feel free to disregard the constitutionally stipulated protocol for amendment. Note that this last condition does not insist that there be widespread agreement on what changes must be made, only widespread agreement that changes must be made and that the constitution is a failed mechanism for making those changes.

Together, these four conditions can be thought of as specifying a limited right of a democratic people, the right to revoke a failed constitutional regime. This is in sharp distinction to the idea that a democratic people enjoy a general right to amend a constitution extraconstitutionally. The requirement of breakdown is meant to respect the representation of the people—the strategy for governing themselves—that they themselves chose in their constitution and have actually lived in their political lives under the constitution. Under anything like ordinary circumstances, the specified means for constitutional amendment should prevail, and questions of constitutional change, including change of the requirements for amending the constitution, ought to be submitted to the people in this privileged form. But when it is widely perceived that the specified means for amending the constitution prevent a necessary constitutional change, and have in contemporary context become a failed representation of the people, the privilege may be revoked.

If the constitution has in fact broken down, members of the political community are once again faced with the menu of choices we considered at the beginning of our constitution-making story: the selection of representatives to a convention or some other mechanism for drafting changes, the voting protocols at the convention stage, the substance of the constitutional changes to be proposed, and the protocol for their acceptance by the polity. The process, whether it aims at relatively modest constitutional changes or complete displacement of the current constitutional scheme, is in an important sense a popular revocation of an at least partially failed constitution; what these choices have in common is the rejection of the specified requirements for constitutional change.

The Puzzle of the Constitution's Birth Revisited

The idea of constitutional breakdown helps to make sense of the otherwise quite puzzling situation of the men who drafted our Constitution and the members of the founding generation who ratified it. On the one hand they asserted and acted upon the proposition that as a democratic people they were entitled to revoke their extant governmental arrangements without following the procedures for change specified in those arrangements. On the other hand, they undertook to bind successive generations to Article V's requirements for amending the Constitution. How could they reconcile the free-form liberty of constitutional choice that they assumed for themselves with the narrow preconditions of constitutional choice that they imposed on the future?

They might have seen themselves as giants and assumed that lesser persons would walk our part of the planet in the future. They might have consciously engaged in an odd kind of political drama, in which the founding generation knows that its successors are fully justified in disregarding their instructions, but nonetheless do their very best to persuade them that this is not the case. Or they might have understood that under the extraordinary circumstances of constitutional breakdown a democratic people have full license to revoke their constitutional arrangements. Only something very much like the distinction between amendment and revocation—with the latter dependent on the widely shared perception of breakdown—can make sense of a thoughtful group of men who apparently believed that a democratic people own their government and can replace it when it becomes necessary, and yet carefully included Article V in their own Constitution.

I do not mean to either assert or deny that the founding generation actually faced constitutional breakdown under the Articles of Confederation, but rather, that we can best make sense out of their views and actions by supposing that they believed themselves at the point of breakdown or something very much like it. The historians among us can no doubt set me right, but I imagine that reasonable persons among the founding generation might well have concluded the following: (a) that sound governance of the nascent republic was impossible under the Articles of Confederation; (b) that meeting the requirements for change under both the Articles of Confederation (which required unanimous state consent) and the respective state constitutions would at best be a process of many years and was quite possibly a doomed venture; and (c) that the representation of the people under the extant regime of law was a failed one in that it made the states rather than the people the units of national government.

If these speculations about the founding generation are true, then the model of breakdown/revocation explains the otherwise odd discrepancy between the ways the founding generation viewed the legal past and the legal future. But I do not mean to belabor or depend upon this possible understanding of history. As we were at some pains to observe early on, the example of the founding generation is only that, and if this attempt to explain that example fails then we may simply have to grant that our constitutional past has its share of warts.

CHAPTER 10

Democracy and the Justice-Seeking Constitution

"Democracy and the Justice-Seeking Constitution" . . . the herald of this, our last chapter, is intentionally loose-limbed. Our concern is only partially and only indirectly the question of whether the justice-seeking account of our constitutional practice is compatible with democracy. To some extent, we have already made our peace with democracy. On the one hand, we have seen that justice-seeking constitutionalism bows to popular political processes twice over: once in denying primary judicial enforcement to constitutional principles that come wrapped with questions of strategy and responsibility that properly belong to popular choice; and then again in shaping the domain of constitutional justice. On the other hand, the democratarian insistence that the exclusive concern of justice-seeking constitutional practice be the improvement of the democratic process has proven unpersuasive, in part on the grounds that democratarian accounts do not enjoy the privileged status against democratic worries that they sometimes seem to claim. Also found unpersuasive was the too-facile claim that in a democracy the people own the constitution and the constitution does not own the people, with the normative consequence that our Constitution's announced protocols for amendment can be disregarded when the people so desire. Thus, much of our discussion to this point has been in the shadow of democratic concerns.

There remain other questions about the democratic bona fides of our constitutional practice, to be sure. But, to a large extent, the most interesting and difficult of these questions are not selective as between the justice-seeking account and even extreme rivals like originalism. Accordingly, much of our attention here will be directed towards the more general question of how our constitutional practice on any plausible account meets democratically inspired criticism. The role of the justice-seeking account in this more general inquiry is importantly positive: Justice-seeking makes much the best sense of robust constitutionalism in the face of democratic doubts.

Court Skepticism

One part politics, one part philosophy, one part a certain perverse academic impulse—whatever the precise recipe, it is the case that just as robust, judicially enforced constitutionalism has become a common feature in almost every modern state throughout the world, and just as even that bastion of parliamentary supremacy, the United Kingdom, is on the brink of embracing constitutionalism,[1] some commentators close to home have begun to favor a world without constitutionally responsible courts. One of these court skeptics is Jeremy Waldron. Waldron thinks judicially enforced constitutionalism is at deep conceptual odds with itself, and that the great swing among democratic states towards judicially enforced constitutional regimes is a fundamental mistake, a mistake that leaves the world much the worse.[2] Waldron's argument is interesting and ingenious. It is also demonstrably wrong—wrong in the best way: When we understand why Waldron is mistaken, we will also

better understand the appeal of judicially enforced constitutionalism to modern democratic states.

Waldron argues that precisely because we think of ourselves as
rights-bearing creatures, we ought to eschew judicial intervention in
our political life on behalf of rights. This apparently paradoxical
argument rests on the claim that there are entailments to the belief
that we are the sorts of creatures that are entitled to rights, and these
entailments are fundamentally inconsistent with judicial deflection
of majoritarian political choices.

Waldron sees two important propositions as entailed by this
important dimension of our self-regard. The first we can call a claim
of *epistemic capacity,* and the second we can call a claim of *deliberative entitlement.*

The claim of epistemic capacity goes roughly like this: If we think
of ourselves as entitled to rights, it follows that we should think of
ourselves as having the capacity to make sound judgments about the
rights we have. If we trust ourselves to exercise the discretion to
choose among courses of action that rights confer upon us, we
ought in turn trust ourselves to reflect upon, debate, and ultimately
come to conclusions about what rights we all have.

We can grant Waldron's conclusion that we should regard ourselves as generally possessed of epistemic capacity with regard to
rights; after all, who besides us is there? But, in passing, we should
note that his particular argument for this capacity is not persuasive.
It does not follow from the fact that we regard ourselves as rights-
worthy that we should regard ourselves as well endowed to make
judgments about rights. We might be the kinds of creatures that are
appropriately seized with rights, especially rights granting us choices
about our own lives, and not be especially good at the enterprise of
self-guidance, although we might be better than anyone else at that
enterprise. And, more to the point, we might be able to make reasonably competent judgments about our own lives yet do poorly

when it comes to the enterprise of charting our collective lives. We might, that is, have good sense with regard to our own projects, but do a bad job of recognizing the claims of others who get in our way.

These difficulties with Waldron's case for epistemic capacity are worth noting, because they help remind us of concerns that will become important further along in the argument, when it comes to applying the premise of epistemic capacity to questions of institutional design, like the choice between legislatures and courts. If, for example, we believe that self-interest may indeed cloud our judgments about the rights that others have, then Waldron's mapping of our commitment to rights onto judgments of epistemic capacity is much too blunt and sweeping, as it ignores the obvious impact of deliberative environments upon our ability to reach sound judgments of many different sorts, including judgments about the rights of others. We will return to this point; for the moment we are getting a little ahead of ourselves.

The second claim that Waldron seeks to derive from the basic fact that we are rights-bearing creatures is one of deliberative entitlement. It is part of the conceptual logic of rights on this account not only that they be *offered* on equal terms but that they be *deliberated* on equal terms. As rights-bearers, insists Waldron, we are all entitled to participate in the process of rights contestation on equal terms. As to this second entailment of rights, I concur. In contestation of rights, we are indeed entitled to be treated as equal members of our political community; and that proposition does seem intrinsic or at least closely connected to the logic of rights.

Let us call these two claims—that we are creatures seized with the capacity to make judgments about rights, and that we are entitled to participate in the process of deliberating about rights on equal terms—Waldron's *primary* arguments. We need a vocabulary of this sort because neither of these claims lends direct support to Waldron's assault on judicially enforced constitutionalism. In each case Waldron needs to turn to a secondary proposition to find support for his ultimate position. And the secondary claims, as we shall see, are where the real difficulty with Waldron's position lies.

From his claim of epistemic capacity, Waldron finds assurance that reasonably well-formed democratic legislatures are trustworthy venues for the contestation of rights, and that we should feel no need to invoke other institutional arrangements, like courts, to improve the outcomes of legislative choice. And from his claim of deliberative entitlement, Waldron concludes that political justice requires parliamentary supremacy and hence bars the intervention of a constitutional judiciary in parliamentary outcomes.

Neither of these secondary claims in fact follows from Waldron's primary claims, and neither is correct. It is just here that Waldron goes wrong, and just here that the instructive force of Waldron's failed argument lies.

Consider the connection between epistemic capacity and the thought that we have no rights-seeking reason to supplement legislative outcomes with judicial oversight. We need at the outset to disabuse ourselves of the picture that seems to lie behind Waldron's argument here, in which the legislature is *us*, and the constitutional judiciary is *them*—an external mechanism intervening in our affairs. The constitutional judiciary, of course, is populated by people just like us—rights-holders, the epistemically endowed. The question has to be under what sorts of circumstances epistemically well-endowed creatures like us are able to do better or worse in the enterprise of making judgments about what rights we should all have. It's not us versus some alien force; it's us in a variety of political and institutional contexts, none of which—on any pertinent axis—is complete or perfect. This much is clear: In debates about fundamental questions of constitutional structure, we are choosing among highly fallible institutional arrangements and looking for those arrangements that have more promise than others. Direct democracy, were it feasible, would comprise one family of contenders; representative parliaments with supreme authority, a second family of contenders; and governments that include a constitutional judiciary with the authority and responsibility of constitutional oversight, a third.

So the question for our present purposes is: Which of these arrangements is more epistemically promising? As we have already been at pains to suggest, there are structural features of a constitutional judiciary that make it a promising environment for the contestation of rights. An appreciation of those features has led an extraordinary number of modern democratic states to adopt written constitutions and empower some judicial entity or entities to enforce those constitutions. Waldron cannot wave aside the epistemic claims on behalf of the judicial enforcement of basic rights on the simple grounds that those rights presuppose the judgmental capacity of our species, full stop. There are at least three qualities of constitutional courts and judges that hold distinct epistemic promise. First, constitutional judges are, in at least two senses, impartial. In most modern constitutional regimes, high court judges are not elected and hence are not vicariously attached to the immediate interests—personal or political—of members of their political community. Moreover (and we will take this up shortly as a matter of independent importance), judges are obliged by the protocols of adjudication to attend to comparatively general and comparatively durable principles—principles that apply to a variety of different circumstances. As a result, judges are affected in a variety of conflicting and diffuse ways by the cases before them. Judges are constrained to abide by principles that, by their temporal, geographic, or substantive reach, sprawl across areas of disinterest and interest on the judges' part. Were they otherwise inclined to choose principles that cut narrowly in favor of things they care about today, they would have to appreciate that those same principles could work powerfully against them tomorrow.

Think, for example, of a judge who is faced with the question of the right of the Ku Klux Klan to burn a cross in a public demonstration. Her ruling on the case will have powerful repercussions in other, easily imaginable cases where she will be much more sympathetic with the would-be demonstrators. So judges are detached twice over—they are detached from the vicarious interests of the members of their political community by the absence of their ongoing political accountability and even from their own immediate interests and projects by the demands of their adjudicatory role.

Second, constitutional judges pursue a function that is specialized and redundant. They are like quality control inspectors in, say, an automobile plant. The job of producing a successful car, after all, is complicated. It certainly includes concerns about the quality of the ultimate product, but it also includes potentially competing concerns, like getting cars out fast and cheaply and producing cars that are attractive. But the quality control inspector has only the job of assuring that the cars which leave her plant are well built. Her role is focused and singular and comes on top of the efforts of the people who actually put the cars together. Constitutional judges are like that. Their mission is singular—to identify the fundamentals of political justice that are prominent and enduring in their constitutional regime and to measure legislation or other governmental acts by those standards. And their mission is redundant—they enter the process only after legislators have themselves considered the constitutional ramifications of proposals before them.

And third, constitutional judges, as an aspect of the practice of common law adjudication, engage in what some philosophers describe as reflective equilibration. A thoughtful judge has to move back and forth between general propositions and specific cases, with the goal of finding those general propositions that seem satisfactory as the basis for her decisions over the run of cases. Judges have to settle on propositions that both account reasonably for past decisions and chart an attractive course for future decisions. This, broadly speaking, is stare decisis doing its job. There are important virtues of this mode of analysis. As we have observed above, the obligation of generality imposed by these adjudicatory constraints serves to create a kind of functional impartiality among judges. Moreover, reflective equilibration is regarded by many moral and political theorists as a natural and effective means of normative reflection, or alternatively, as a means to check or discipline normative reflection.

Law students are familiar with this process, which often goes something like this. Professor offers hypothetical, asks how the case —involving, say, landmark preservation restraints on a landowner— should be decided and why. Student replies, offering in part a general principle, like "Whenever the government causes a landowner to suffer a diminution in the value of her land, the government should be obliged to compensate the owner." Professor offers an instance where the student's principle is likely to produce what the student will regard as undesirable results: "Suppose the government builds a new highway, which has the effect of enticing traffic away from the little town where the owner owns a gas station, and the owner loses a lot of income and suffers a diminution in the value of her land?" Student replies, offering a better-shaped principle, possibly even changing her mind about the appropriate outcome in the original hypothetical. And so on.

There is as well a deeper reason for favoring the common law model of adjudication as a means of deliberating about rights. Much modern thinking about political morality—often described as contractualist thought—has in common the idea that our political arrangements must in principle be justifiable from the perspective of each member of the political community. And, more broadly, it is an intrinsic aspect of the substantive logic of rights that they be available to everyone who falls within their substantive reach; in this sense, the notion of equal rights is redundant. Generalization is thus at the substantive heart of sound deliberation about rights. The institutionalized process of reflective equilibration, towards which common law adjudication aims, instantiates this moral demand for generalization.

Constitutional judges are emphatically not a natural or constructed elite, endowed with unquestionable expertise. But their role —their function—may well give them a distinct epistemic advantage.

Waldron's other crucial secondary claim is derived from his claim of deliberative entitlement. His claim here is that it follows from the right of equal participation in the contestation of rights that members of a just political community are entitled to an elected legislature that has final authority over the content of contested rights.

In thinking about this, it is important to consider two very different ways in which people can participate as equals in the process of deliberating about rights.

One way in which a member of a political community can participate as an equal in the process of resolving disputes over what rights members of that community have is by being equally entitled to vote for political representatives, who will in turn make decisions about rights. This is certainly not an unimportant way to participate in rights contestation, but it is in some respects a thin way and a dangerous way. It is thin and dangerous because elected political representatives are inevitably drawn in some not insubstantial degree to respond to the power of votes or of dollars as opposed to the force of an individual's or group's claim that they have right on their side.

The second way that a member of a political community can participate as an equal in the process of rights contestation is to have her rights and interests—as an equal member of the political community and as an equal rights-holder—seriously considered and taken account of by those in deliberative authority. Any member of the community is entitled, on this account, to have each deliberator assess her claims on its merits, notwithstanding the number of votes that stand behind her, notwithstanding how many dollars she is able to deploy on her behalf, and notwithstanding what influence she has in the community. Implicit in this form of equal participation is the right to be heard and to be responded to in terms that locate each person's claim of rights against the backdrop of the community's broad commitment to and understanding of the rights that all members have.

Legislatures, obviously, are preferred venues for the first mode— the *electoral* mode—of participating as equals in the process of choosing among conflicting views of what rights we should all have. Less obviously, perhaps, courts are preferred venues for the *deliberative* mode of participating in that process. Any person injured in the right sort of way is entitled to be heard by courts, entitled to present her claims and the arguments on their behalf, and, at worst, entitled to a reasoned statement of why her claims were not deemed by a majority of the judges to be persuasive. Judges may well be flawed deliberators, of course, and the very independence that makes them impartial also makes them relatively impervious to electoral correction. But when a constitutional protagonist turns to the courts, she can be anyone; she can represent a minority of one or be a member of a group that is widely ridiculed or deplored. Much of what is good in constitutional law, in fact, has been provoked by the claims of such groups. What matters is the strength of her argument in the eyes of the judges, and, failing her success, she is entitled to an explanation of why her claim was found wanting.

Many contemporary democratic theorists argue for a political process that combines both electoral and deliberative equality in the process of rights contestation. Frequently proceeding under the banner of "deliberative democracy," these theorists sometimes conjure an idealized legislative process in which elected representatives in effect hear and resolve the conflicting claims and competing interests of all the individuals in the community, are conscientious and articulate in their adjudication of those claims, and cast their votes on the proposals before them in accord with their best understanding of what each claimant is owed.

Common to this line of democratic thought is the starting point that members of a democratic community must treat each other as equals. From this stipulation there flow two others: Each member of the community must have an opportunity to be heard—in the strong sense of having his or her arguments taken seriously for what they are worth, without regard to his or her power or position—on each contested question of community choice; and each member of the community should support only those community choices that he or she believes are reasonable from the vantage of every other member of the community regarded as an equal. Even if this idealized account could be realized in practice, of course, there would almost certainly be substantial disagreements. But these would be disagreements of a particular sort: They would be disagreements about what was the right thing to do. Deliberation followed by a vote would produce "a pooling of judgments," not a "vector sum" of aggregated preferences.[3] The majority would win, but by the post-deliberation assemblage of individual judgments; and in this sense, at least, it would be "reason" rather than "power" that would prevail.

As a purely theoretical matter, there is some question as to whether a single representative or body of representatives can simultaneously do justice to the demands of both electoral and deliberative equality. But setting that interesting question aside for another day, it plainly is the case that modern legislatures are structured to respond to electoral rather than deliberative responsibility, and that the deliberative legislative assembly is at best a conceptual goal rather than a practical reality.

The structure of popular political institutions seems better suited to the negotiated summation of preferences than the deliberative pooling of judgments. This is not a circumstance that should be greeted with dismay, since the competition for support will often push the powerful to include the interests of the less powerful in their political agendas. Driven in part by their location at the margins of power, "discrete and insular minorities" may through coordination of their determined energy acquire genuine political muscle.[4] But this is a function of what is expedient in shifting political circumstances, of the wavering hand of a process that is not accidental, but which proceeds far more readily by the logic of accumulated power than by that of reflective justice. No one can demand to be heard or to have their interests taken into account unless they can make themselves strategically valuable. In the real world of popular politics, power, not truth, speaks to power.

Courts, of course, are far from perfect, and I do not mean to invite the comparison of the real world of popular politics—its blemishes made prominent—with a Pollyannaish vision of the constitutional judiciary at its best. The point, though, is this: Popular politics and constitutionalism represent fundamentally different faces of democracy, different democratic modalities. In an important sense, these two institutional arrangements aspire to different democratic virtues. To be sure, no society without a robust place for popular politics can be counted as democratic or just. And it may be sensible to speak of trade-offs between these democratic virtues in the course of institutional design. But it is a mistake to think that there is a blunt opposition between process and outcome—between the fair and democratic process of popular politics and the potential for just results offered by robust judicial constitutionalism. Constitutional adjudication embodies a distinct process that is itself fair and democratic, fair and democratic in a way that popular political institutions cannot realistically be.

Most modern democratic states now have a portfolio of institutional arrangements in which legislatures offer the promise of electoral equality and constitutional courts offer the promise of deliberative equality. No governmental arrangements are anything near perfect, of course, and we can no doubt find much to criticize and much to improve upon in both contemporary legislatures and contemporary constitutional courts. And it is too early in modern democratic history to say that a political community that includes judicially enforced constitutionalism in its portfolio of governing mechanisms is inherently better off for having done so. But it is surely a mistake to conclude a priori that a society that maintains a pure system of legislative supremacy better respects its citizens as rights-holders and political equals than one which makes rights the center of a judicially enforced constitutional practice.

Suppose that Britain still maintained its historic structure of governance, which to a modern constitutionalist looks remarkably nonconstitutional, with no written constitution and no interference by the judiciary with the will of the Parliament in the name of enduring practices and values of the sort we associate with the U.S. Constitution. And suppose further that an exhaustive inventory revealed that, bracketing the question of parliamentary sovereignty versus judicial review in the name of the Constitution, Britain and the United States were identical in their conformity with the fundamental requirements of political justice. Now the question is this: Would we be tempted to say that Britain, which got to be as it is without the intervention of a constitutional judiciary, was for that reason the more just (or at least the more democratic) political community? It seems a small concession: We could say yes and speak of England's unique cultural history as a tight little island, note the impossibly counterfactual nature of the complicated inventory of political justice, and gesture towards a trade-off of process and results in our own experience as a constitutional democracy. It would be a small concession, but it would be wrong; a democratic state is if anything enriched in coin of democracy itself by the inclusion of a constitutionally responsible judiciary within its portfolio of governing institutions.[5]

Democratic Restraint and Deliberative Integrity

The lesson of our excursion into court skepticism has important consequences for a more modest and more subtle claim—a claim for the shading of judicial constitutionalism rather than its abandonment. The claim, broadly, is this: Democratic principle and/or institutional prudence give the Supreme Court good reason to minimize the conflict between its decisions and contrary views widely held among the citizens of our political community. It is perhaps a mistake to see this as a single claim; there is a family of claims that are recognizably connected to this idea of democratic restraint. Taken together, this family has a powerful grip on contemporary scholarly reflection on our constitutional practice.

Claims from within this family are not necessarily antagonistic to the justice-seeking account of our constitutional practice. To the contrary, the idea of democratic restraint is best understood as coming from within the justice-seeking account, and its sponsors often make explicit use of justice-seeking resources, including the idea that there is an appropriate gap between the reach of constitutional justice and the reach of the constitutional doctrine. But there are reasons why we should be slow to welcome the democratic restraint inflection of the justice-seeking account.

We can consider these reasons against the backdrop of one of the most plausible and attractive versions of the democratic restraint thesis; I have in mind the work of Richard Fallon. Fallon writes:

[T]he Justices' work in interpreting the Constitution and in crafting implementing doctrine must be rooted in values that can reasonably be viewed as shared. Without surrendering its prerogatives of judgment or compromising its obligation to uphold constitutional values in the face of political opposition, the Court, in specifying the *meaning* of constitutional principles, must be accountable at least in part to manifestations of reasonable moral and political commitments displayed by the citizenry, both nationally and locally.[6]

So put, Fallon's claim is tentative in its reach. The most vivid example he offers does not go far in giving his thesis a firm edge. The Supreme Court, he suggests, was right in unanimously rejecting the claim that there is a constitutional right to physician-assisted suicide, and this is so even if any given justice would have correctly believed that the best, internal, moral reading of the Constitution includes such a right. Such a justice would be unfaithful to her role if she "prematurely spoke the truth as [she] personally saw it, and crafted bad doctrine that frustrated reasoned debate and democratic experiment."[7]

There are several features of the assisted-suicide cases that make them particularly appealing for Fallon's purposes (and which, for similar reasons, may leave important questions unanswered). First, and perhaps most importantly, the area of physician-assisted suicide is dominated by practical concerns the resolution of which may well be better and more appropriately handled by legislative experiments at the state level. Second, there are four or possibly five justices in these cases who declined to intervene in the pertinent state law regimes, but went to some pains to leave open the possibility that the Court would be obliged in some time, place, and circumstance to intervene on behalf of some form of the right to die with dignity and without undue suffering.[8] Had these justices more clearly prevailed, these cases would be instances of explicit and provisional under-enforcement of the Constitution, pursuant to which its meaning would not be compromised. (In contrast, the "majority" of the Court offered a crabbed and implausible view about the meaning of the Constitution in this area.) Third, this is an area largely uncharted by constitutional experience, precedent, or other comforting guides to constitutional meaning. And fourth, this is an area of law involving the immediate or prospective experience of virtually every member of the political community, an area in which, accordingly, we can expect state legislatures and engaged state populations to pursue rather than deflect justice and compassion, and an area in which we in fact do see that pursuit in action.

But suppose we posit a case where a conflict of constitutional meaning is presented more sharply. Suppose we imagine the Supreme Court confronts the question of whether same-sex couples are constitutionally entitled to be married.[9] Now Fallon's counsel seems to have considerably more—and considerably more troubling—bite:

> Although constitutional adjudicators cannot be paralyzed by reasonable disagreement, they must take into account their capacity to function effectively as representative decision-makers, whose judgments should exercise at least some influence, over time, on the moral consciences of those who might immediately be inclined to disagree. In light of recent experience, notably with respect to *Roe v. Wade*, the current Supreme Court has good reason to doubt its capacity to lead moral opinion effectively if it were to push too far ahead of prevailing sentiment with respect to many controverted issues.[10]

Fallon seems to invite a wide, all-things-considered judgment by the Court as to the question of whether it can "effectively . . . lead moral opinion" with respect to a potentially controversial outcome in a case before it. It bears emphasis that Fallon is driven by principle, not prudence. Specifically, he is concerned about "the fair allocation of political power." This can only deepen the seriousness of what Fallon is proposing. His counsel would encourage the Court to regard widespread opposition to the legal recognition of homosexual relationships as undermining the propriety of finding that the Constitution gives gays and lesbians the right to marry.

We should note in passing that the case of gay marriage, like many other highly controversial constitutional issues, cannot be tamed by insisting that the Court's role is limited to the concrete implementation of widely shared first principles of political justice. On many views—including my own—the anti-caste principle that is at the heart of our commitment to constitutional equality ought to be understood as giving the Court a good reason to vigorously protect the rights of gays and lesbians. Certainly one could believe that and still observe the fact of widespread controversy over gay rights in general and same-sex marriage in particular. No justice who believed that something like the anti-caste principle was one of the essential precepts of constitutional justice would be acting on her own maverick beliefs. She could rightly conclude both that this idea has a venerable pedigree in the work of the modern Court and that it is widely endorsed in our political community. It is thus emphatically true that the case on behalf of the right of gays and lesbians to marry is "rooted in values that reasonably can be viewed as shared." But this merely makes the stakes of democratic restraint especially high; it seems unlikely that any of the proponents of democratic restraint would be satisfied that the Court should plunge ahead on these grounds alone.

In the face of widespread social controversy, on what grounds can the morally precocious judge pronounce the disagreement she faces "reasonable," or for that matter, "unreasonable"? If we consider cases like physician-assisted suicide or campaign finance restrictions, we can see a special sense in which disagreement can be reasonable: In these cases, people with very much the same idea of what is importantly at stake in the enterprise of constitutional justice can find themselves disagreeing about social strategy. But in cases like abortion rights, or gay marriage, or school prayer, there are sharp issues of principle which divide the heated protagonists on both sides, however much sharing of root fundamental values there might otherwise be between them. Is reasonability a matter of how certain each judge is of his or her constitutional judgment? That would seem to make it a matter of cognitive personality.

Perhaps the idea is one of core and penumbra: The idea would be that each side agrees on clear cases of what does or does not violate, say, the anti-caste principle, and could even agree on what cases were unclear. On this account, there could be widespread agreement that a given case fell in the unclear margins of a constitutional precept; disagreement about such a marginal case would perforce be reasonable. But in precisely those cases where widespread controversy threatens a constitutional judgment by the Court, each side will see the judgment of its opposite as unreasonable as well as wrong.

But these are preliminary matters. The most troubling aspect of the democratic restraint thesis runs deeper. When Alex Bickel argued that the constitutional judiciary should duck politically inconvenient cases—most notably those in which a court's commitment to general principles would require it validate a socially objectionable law[11]—Gerald Gunther demurred. Gunther objected that Bickel's assertion amounted to "100 per cent insistence on principle, 20 per cent of the time."[12] His point was simple and important: If in some important sense the constitutional judiciary's legitimacy depends upon its principled behavior, then a prescription for part-time principle is deeply suspect.

The relevance of our encounter with court skepticism should now be obvious. The democratic stature of constitutional adjudication is in important part dependent upon the deliberative promise of the judicial forum. Ideally, every claimant before a court stands on equal footing; the force of his or her claim is the force of reason— the strength of its connection to an articulate scheme of principle—

not of wealth, popularity, or social stature. The epistemic efficacy of constitutional adjudication is similarly dependent. In the course of deciding a case before them, judges are responsible to both past decisions and future possibilities; they must test the principles upon which they are tempted to rely against these other outcomes, real and imagined, and they are obliged to give each other and the broader audience of their opinions reasons for their decisions. These are all crucial features of the deliberative aspects of adjudication.

Consider how deeply this picture is compromised if we take it to be a welcome or even required feature of constitutional adjudication that judges pull their punches in controversial cases. How is a constitutional court's decision in a gay marriage case to read, when—as we are for these purposes assuming—the court is convinced both that the anti-caste principle demands that homosexuals be entitled to marry and that significant numbers of persons in our political community are strongly opposed to that conclusion? Should the court announce that gays and lesbians are, in its judgment, being denied what one of the Constitution's most important principles entitles them too, but that its role stops at the edge of deep political controversy? Should the court instead misstate the scope and application of the anti-caste principle? Should the court simply be magisterially opaque? And how, if either of the latter two courses is prescribed, should the court behave in its next case involving the scope and application of the anti-caste principle—by simply ignoring its prior gay marriage decision?—by reshaping its anti-caste jurisprudence to suit that decision?

The issue is one of institutional integrity. Judges who play politics are in an important sense not acting as judges. Deliberation compromised by a thick overlay of political caution is in danger of losing much of its value as deliberation. It is hard to conceive of an open and articulate regime in which judges routinely and self-consciously share their decisional responsibilities on an all-things-considered basis with as diffuse a force as the judges' sense of the breadth and intensity of contrary public opinion. Yet that seems precisely the course argued for by the political restraint thesis, even in the hands of its most thoughtful and capable expositors.

This is not to say that constitutional adjudication must be taken on an all or nothing basis. We still have ahead a discussion of whether the obduracy to constitutional change enforced by the amendment requirements of Article V effectuates what Richard Fallon worries is an unfair distribution of political power. But let us suppose for the moment that we become persuaded that his concern is well placed, and that political justice would be better served if members of our political community had more of a voice in decisions about controversial questions of political justice than is available to them under our constitutional practice as it stands. Were we designing an institutional regime from scratch, or disposed to think about major changes in our own institutional arrangements, we could make space for that voice without compromising the judicial process. We could adjust the amendment rules. We could provide for a congressional override of Supreme Court decisions under appropriate circumstances calculated to induce popular input and careful congressional reflection—we could, for example, provide for majority or supermajority override upon two congressional votes with an intervening national election.

All of these possibilities carry with them advantages and disadvantages, and I have already devoted a fair amount of ink and argument in these pages on behalf of the often unobserved virtues of both Article V and the process of constitutional adjudication. And we are about to absolve Article V of at least the harshest democratic complaints lodged against it. So I am not inclined to step quickly aboard any of these bandwagons. But it is important to note that mechanisms of these sorts have the distinct advantage of preserving the deliberative integrity of the constitutional judiciary.

Article V, Constitutional Obduracy, and Democracy

In our earlier discussion of constitutional birth and amendment, we left open the question of whether Article V so distorts or muffles the popular voice as to undermine the democratic bona fides of our constitutional practice. On the account implied by this worry, the perfectly democratic constitution would be open to something approaching revisability by simple majority vote. As you move away from this benchmark towards requirements that make the Constitution strongly obdurate to change, you place a constitutional regime at greater and greater odds with the democratic ideal.

The Article V critic who takes this line is appealing to our deep sense that in a democracy the people rule, and, as a corollary, the less well-considered proposition that rule by the people entails simple majority vote. But, as we have seen, the idea of the popular sovereign is at best a metaphor, and here, as is often the case in constitutional discourse, that metaphor obscures rather than reveals many important questions. Every protocol for popular judgment is at best one possible depiction of the distribution of preferences, judgments, and sensibilities among the people as a whole.

The claim that the obduracy of constitutional outcomes in our practice—an obduracy for which Article V is in no small measure responsible—is anathema to democracy, accordingly, must depend on more than simple arithmetic or convention. Considerably more is required before we can accept the claim that a well-formed democratic community must have as one of its features something approaching majority control over its constitutive arrangements. And the more must come from within—be a claim sounding in—constitutional justice. What could an argument to this effect rely on?

In our discussion of the domain of constitutional justice in chapter 8, we identified four fundamental concerns of political justice, two of which seem particularly salient to the claim that democracy insists on the revisability of important political choices by something approaching simple majority vote. They are *equal membership,* which requires that the interests and concerns of all groups and persons within our political community be treated with the same regard as the interests and concerns of all other groups and persons; and *fair and open government,* which requires that the processes of government be fair to all members of our political community and open to their participation and voice. The Article V critic could appeal to each. The equal membership argument would insist that only simple majority rule treats each person equally, since any other voting protocol cedes to some minority the capacity to block the will of the majority, and this must mean that the votes of those in the minority count for more. The fair and open government argument would insist that the obduracy of the constitutional results to revision serves to exclude the voice of contemporary political majorities. We can take these up in turn.

In thinking about equality of membership and the resistance of the Constitution to amendment, it is useful at the outset to observe the distinction between the distribution of agency and the differential weighing of votes. The formidable Article V requirement of ratification by three-fourths of the states is a distribution of agency, and it is distinctly odd to object to it as a failure of equal regard. Consider the requirement in municipal law that a community's effort to annex a particular area be supported by electoral majorities in both the annexing community and the target area. Suppose that the annexation is strongly supported by the voters in the annexing community, but rejected by a majority of the much smaller electorate in the target area. We could characterize the annexation rule as a unanimity requirement, since both electoral entities must agree; and it would be true that a comparatively small number of voters could defeat the will of a much larger group. But the voters in the target area are not being preferred in any illuminating sense of that verb; they are merely being accorded agency over their own municipal destiny.

True, Article V makes it harder to amend the Constitution than would other possible rules, including a majority vote among the entire national electorate, or a more or less ordinary legislative act by Congress standing alone; and true, the mutual-agreement-to-annexation rule makes it harder to annex a target area than would other possible rules. But that does not of itself give rise to complaint, and if either of these rules is objectionable for this reason alone, the objection must be based on something other than equal membership.

Perhaps the relevant comparison is not between Article V and other possible voting protocols, but rather between possible outcomes under Article V. Certainly it requires a much broader base of support to amend the Constitution than to defeat a proposed amendment. Because the population of the fifty states varies so radically, it is not possible to measure the differential burden in terms of numbers of voters, but the differential is very great, and under many plausible scenarios, comparatively few voters could indeed defeat a constitutional amendment.

This suggests a second distinction, implicated by the distinction between the differential weighing of votes and the distribution of agency—namely, the distinction between disfavoring persons and disfavoring positions. Any voting regime that disfavors persons is suspect on equal membership grounds, and requires a substantial justification. But a voting regime that disfavors positions is not of itself in tension with equal membership. Depending on its form and rationale, we might consider a position-disfavoring vote rule a good or bad thing, but without more, our concern about such a rule would not turn on equality of membership. This is true even of straightforward supermajority rules where the differential burden on those favoring the nondefault position is concrete and quantifiable in terms of the number of voters required to overcome that burden.

There may be situations in which the interests of some classes of persons or groups are so deeply and pathologically associated with some issues that a position-favoring rule would be inconsistent with equal membership. This would be true, for example in a society (Oklahomia?) where there was a durable distinction between farmers and ranchers. We imagine that the ranchers dominate in their wealth and stature; that mobility between the careers is as a practical matter difficult; that ranchers require open ranges to thrive; and that farmers, conversely, require fences. In such a society, a voting rule which made open ranges the default and required a supermajority vote as a precondition to any permission to fence might well be an affront to equal regard. But this functional inequality of membership is a special case, born of special circumstances; the mere formal disfavoring of a position does not put equal membership at hazard.

On the contrary, a voting protocol that formally disfavors a position may functionally improve equality of membership. That is precisely what we have to hope from the rigors of Article V. The insistence on a supermajority of states is a reasonable proxy for the demand that constitutional precepts be acceptable to persons in a wide variety of circumstances, while the general difficulty of amending the Constitution causes popular constitutional decision-makers to take account of their own future interests and those of their children and their children's children—all of which should conduce towards the selection of constitutional principles fair to all members in the community. There may be other ways of organizing a well-formed and well-functioning democratic community, but the amendment strategy of Article V is a reasonably promising mechanism to that end. In any event, it is hard to see how an amendment protocol like that of Article V is inconsistent with equality of membership.

That leaves the charge that our constitutional practice, regulated as it is by Article V, is unacceptable simply because it interferes too drastically with the ability of the people to control their government, that it inappropriately muffles the democratic voice. Here again, the lesson of our reflections on court skepticism is crucial: In modern democratic states, participation—we could just as aptly speak of voice—comes in two distinct forms, electoral and deliberative. Both have distinct and distinctly democratic virtues.

Article V's obduracy, we have seen, conduces to a constitutional text that is general and abstract as well as obdurate, and thus creates space for deliberation by constitutional courts; in so doing, Article V creates space for deliberative participation in the process of rights contestation. To be sure, it does so at the expense of the increased opportunity for electoral participation in rights contestation that a more freely amendable constitution would offer. But this trade-off among modes of democratic participation cannot be faulted a priori on grounds that it muffles the democratic voice.

Consider a governmental regime in which there is a constitution, but it is relatively easy to amend. The constitution in this regime, not surprisingly, is relatively prolix and detailed, reflecting both the availability of amendment and actual frequent resort to amendment by plebiscite and/or legislation. We do not have to conjure such a regime from whole cloth: Many state constitutions bear at least some resemblance to this stylized regime. California's constitution, for example, has been amended over five hundred times and runs to some four thousand pages. In such a regime, the line between constitutional provisions and ordinary legislation remains, but is blurred; and in such a regime, electoral participation in the shaping of constitutional content is greatly increased. But in such a regime the range of judicial judgment over questions of constitutional substance is substantially foreshortened, and so too is deliberative participation. There is nothing abstract about the trade-off between electoral and deliberative participation here. A high court decision granting gays and lesbians the right to marry is far more vulnerable to electoral reversal in this regime.

This is not to say, of course, that the balance between electoral and deliberative participation in the process of rights contestation is arbitrary or irrelevant to the well-being of a political community. Nor is it possible on the strength of these observations and our earlier extensive discussion of Article V to say that Article V is un-flawed, or even that its terms compose the most suitable arrange-ment for the United States, all things considered. But the substantial virtues we have identified in Article V are contributions to a distinct and valuable form of democratic participation, and that is the cru-cial point overlooked by the charge that Article V's obduracy threat-ens the democratic bona fides of our constitutional practice.

The Instrumental Claim for Electoral Participation

The justice-seeking account of our constitutional practice might nevertheless be faulted for its celebration of judicial deliberation at the expense of popular electoral contestation of rights. The argu-ment might go something like this: The best constitution and the best judges cannot save a democratic people from their own folly or mean-spiritedness. Only an ongoing moral commitment by an en-gaged people can in the end succeed in the enterprise of maintaining fidelity to justice. Justice-seeking constitutionalism itself recognizes this when it assigns constitutional justice a restricted domain within political justice, and restricts judicial enforcement of constitutional justice to a still narrower domain. What the justice-seeking account fails to recognize is that the moral muscle of the American people has atrophied precisely because we have ceded to judges the respon-sibility for deciding critical issues of political justice. In this way, the justice-seeking approach has done damage to our capacity as a people to do justice, a capacity upon which we must ultimately depend.

There may be reason to despair at the moral tone of contemporary political life, and it is certainly tempting to find a whipping boy like the constitutional judiciary to which we can assign responsibility for our collective failure of responsibility. But this assignment is simply and drastically wrong.

To begin with, no sensible observer could imagine that the issues of justice in our political life have been exhausted by a rapacious constitutional judiciary. Judicial enforcement of the precepts of constitutional justice occupies only a small corner of the modern moral landscape that we as a people must traverse. We are literally surrounded by burning questions of our responsibility to redress the entrenched and skewed distribution of wealth and opportunity; of our obligation to the very young and the very old, neither of whom can fend for themselves; of the justness of our regime of taxation; of the environment and the nature and extent of our obligation to future generations; of the character of our obligation to intervene in the affairs of other nations when deep and tragic injustices occur; of the conditions under which it is just to make war, and the expedients that war may or may not justify. And on and on. . . . If our political life has slighted these issues or their moral dimension, that is our fault, not the fault of the constitutional judiciary. If our moral muscle has atrophied, that is because we are political couch potatoes; there is more than enough room for exercise.

Nor could a sensible observer of our political life conclude that those matters which do get taken up by the judiciary in the name of the Constitution are thereby swept off the popular political agenda. Our actual experience suggests just the opposite. Constitutional decisions shape and crystallize the underlying questions of principle, and seem if anything to galvanize popular concern. Consider our modern constitutional experience: the school prayer cases and the

Native American peyote decision; *Brown v. Board of Education; Roe v. Wade*[13] and its progeny; the sex discrimination cases from *Reed v. Reed*[14] through the VMI decision; *Bowers v. Hardwick, Romer v. Evans,* and now *Lawrence v. Texas;* speech decisions implicating hate speech, pornography, flag-burning and campaign financing; the budding federalism decisions that led to a modest bloom in *Lopez;* or the recent decisions on affirmative action and racial districting. These include, I imagine, the cases on almost everyone's hit parade and hit list. It would have been silly in prospect to think that these cases could lay the social controversies with which they contended to rest, and utterly wrong in retrospect to think that they have done so. In some instances the Supreme Court has been a foil for dissent or legislative response; in some, an organizer of contentious disagreement; and, in still others, the author of a definitive conceptual vocabulary by which discourse and analysis can proceed. In all, these cases have, if anything, made the American people more alert to the issues of political justice that lie just beneath the surface of these controversies.

Conclusion

In June of 2003, when the manuscript for this book was in train, the Supreme Court decided *Lawrence v. Texas.*[1] In *Lawrence,* the Court was confronted by a Texas law that described particular acts of sexual intimacy between persons of the same sex as "[d]eviate sexual intercourse,"[2] and made engaging in those acts a criminal offense. In a sweeping decision, the Court held the Texas law unconstitutional:

> [This] case . . . involve[s] two adults who, with full and mutual consent from each other, engaged in sexual practices common to a homosexual lifestyle. The petitioners are entitled to respect for their private lives. The State cannot demean their existence or control their destiny by making their private sexual conduct a crime. Their right to liberty under the Due Process Clause gives them the full right to engage in their conduct without intervention of the government. "It is a promise of the Constitution that there is a realm of personal liberty which the government may not enter." The Texas statute furthers no legitimate state interest which can justify its intrusion into the personal and private life of the individual.[3]

Five justices joined the Court's opinion, which was authored by Justice Kennedy. In the course of its opinion, the Court flatly overruled its prior decision in *Bowers v. Hardwick*,[4] which had upheld a Georgia statute outlawing sodomy against a Due Process Clause challenge. A sixth member of the Court, Justice O'Connor, supported the decision on Equal Protection Clause grounds, and would not have overruled *Bowers*.

The Court in *Lawrence* did not argue that the text or history of the Fifth or Fourteenth Amendment would spontaneously yield the conclusion that the Texas law was unconstitutional. Nor did the Court argue that an enactment-centered dig into the history of the amendments would produce a concrete nub of meaning which, when suitably translated to our time and place, or appropriately combined with other layers of constitutional substance, would demand that conclusion. Instead, the Court said this: "Had those who drew and ratified the Due Process Clauses of the Fifth Amendment or the Fourteenth Amendment known the components of liberty in its manifold possibilities, they might have been more specific. They did not presume to have this insight. They knew times can blind us to certain truths and later generations can see that laws once thought necessary and proper in fact serve only to oppress. As the Constitution endures, persons in every generation can invoke its principles in their own search for greater freedom."[5]

Nor did the Court in *Lawrence* bend to the chore of aligning its judgment with the process of democratic choice. For the *Lawrence* Court, the right of gays and lesbians to live free and dignified lives did not derive from the goal of making it possible for gays and lesbians to perform authentic roles as active members of our political community; nor did that right turn on the nice question of whether the demands of free and equal citizenship are part of the requirements of democracy itself or, rather, are fundamentals of political justice that lie alongside the requirements of democracy.

What the Court in *Lawrence* turned to, ultimately, were compelling principles of liberty and equality rooted in its own jurisprudence, spawned in the course of decades of its justice-seeking enterprise. Setting aside the false step of *Bowers*, from *Griswold v. Connecticut*[6] onwards the Court had implicitly recognized that choices of adults concerning the intimate details of their consensual, privately conducted sexual relationships were presumptively outside the reach of state authority. A state whose only warrant for intervention in such choices was the view of a legislative majority that the conduct in question was immoral could not constitutionally interfere with those choices. That tradition was the basis of the *Lawrence* Court's due process conclusion. Further, while declining to rule on equal protection grounds, the Court went out of its way to suggest that the proper understanding of due process entailed many of the concerns traditionally associated with constitutional equality. In the relevant passages, the Court speaks of the "due process right to demand respect" for protected conduct, arguing that "[w]hen homosexual conduct is made criminal," that alone is a source of "stigma" and may function "as an invitation to subject homosexual persons to discrimination in the public and in the private spheres." This deployment of equality reasons for the Court's due process ruling culminates in the observation that the continued existence of *Bowers* as good law in and of itself "demeans homosexual persons." In all, there is an unmistakable echo of the anthem sounded in the elder Justice Harlan's dissent in *Plessy v. Ferguson*: "There is no caste here."[7]

The *Lawrence* decision was not an affront to democracy. The process that generated the decision offered conditions of deliberative equality that no legislature could reliably promise. When the claims of John Geddes Lawrence and Tyron Garner were presented to the Court, what mattered was not the number of electoral votes that sponsored them, nor the amount of financial or political support that would be mobilized in response to a decision favoring their position. What mattered was whether they could successfully appeal to the scheme of principle developed in the course of the Court's efforts to discern, articulate, and respond to the fundamental demands of political justice. It is no democratic vice for a political community to provide its members the deliberative forum of a constitutional court.

Any thought that the *Lawrence* decision will somehow sap the political arena of moral energy is far-fetched in the extreme. As of this writing, matters are far from settled. In the wake of *Lawrence*, the Supreme Judicial Court of Massachusetts held that the Massachusetts constitution "affirms the dignity and equality of all individuals," and that, accordingly, the state may not "deny the protections, benefits, and obligations conferred by civil marriage to two individuals of the same sex who wish to marry."[8] *Lawrence* is cited early and prominently in the court's opinion, and may have helped encourage the outcome. Together, *Lawrence* and the Massachusetts decision— *Goodridge v. Department of Public Health*—have placed the debate over the rights and stature of gays and lesbians squarely on the national public agenda.

The *Lawrence* decision is a momentous event in our constitutional history. It promises an era in which the incomplete project of welcoming gays and lesbians into our political community is finally realized. And it reflects the willingness of the men and women who sit as justices on the Supreme Court to shoulder the burdens of moral judgment when legal events so demand. Arguably, it is the most important decision since *Brown v. Board of Education*. But, in one sense, it is business as usual. It is justice in plainclothes.

Notes

Acknowledgments

1. "Justice in Plain Clothes: Reflections on the Thinness of Constitutional Law," 88 *Northwestern University Law Review* 410 (1993). Portions of this essay are included in the discussion of the moral shortfall of constitutional law and judicial underenforcement of the Constitution in Chapters 5, 6, and 7.

2. "The Betrayal of Judgment," 65 *Fordham Law Review* 1545 (1997). A portion of this small essay is adapted to introduce reluctant judgment theory in Chapter 4.

3. "Fair Measure: The Legal Status of Underenforced Constitutional Norms," 91 *Harvard Law Review* 1212 (1978). Portions of this essay are included in the discussion of underenforcement in Chapter 6.

4. "A Letter to the Supreme Court Regarding the Missing Argument in Brzonkala v. Morrison," 75 *New York University Law Review* 150 (2000). A portion of this small essay is adapted for use in the Chapter 7 discussion of remedial underenforcement.

5. "Constitutional Justice," 6 *New York Journal of Legislation and Public Policy* 11 (2002–3). An adapted version of this small essay is used in the critique of Jeremy Waldron in Chapter 10.

6. Chapter 8 derives from "The Domain of Constitutional Justice," in *Constitutionalism—Philosophical Foundations* (Larry Alexander ed., Cambridge University Press 1998). Chapter 9 and a small portion of Chapter 10 derive from "The Birth Logic of a Democratic Constitution," in *Constitutional Culture and Democratic Rule* (John Ferejohn, Jack N. Rakove, and Jonathan Riley eds., Cambridge University Press 2003).

Introduction

1. Since 1990, following on the heels of the Supreme Court's decision in *Texas v. Johnson,* 491 U.S. 391 (1989), Congress has been flirting with the possibility of proposing an amendment that would permit the banning of flag burning as a means of political protest. The House has voted by the required two-thirds majority to recommend the "Flag Protection Amendment" on several occasions, but the Senate has consistently averted granting its two-thirds support, albeit by a close margin on at least one occasion. Similarly, since the Court's decision outlawing official prayer in public schools in *Engel v. Vitale,* 370 U.S. 421 (1962), periodic efforts to amend the Constitution in service of a vision of religious liberty substantially at odds with the Court's have surfaced and made some headway.

2. Bruce Ackerman and Akhil Reed Amar have both argued that extra-Article V efforts to amend the Constitution are valid. I take up their arguments in Chapter 9, under the heading of "The Birth Logic of a Democratic Constitution."

3. Barry Friedman documented the history of these objections to the working of the Court at great length. See, e.g., Barry Friedman, "The History of the Countermajoritarian Difficulty, Part Four: Law's Politics," 148 *University of Pennsylvania Law Review* 971 (2000); Barry Friedman, "The History of the Countermajoritarian Difficulty, Part One: The Road to Judicial Supremacy," 73 *New York University Law Review* 333 (1998).

4. Jeremy Waldron is a prominent example of the school who believe that it is too late to imagine that the United States will see the light and change course away from our constitutional practice. His arguments against judicially enforced constitutional practice are introduced and addressed in Chapter 10, under the heading of "Democracy and the Justice-Seeking Constitution."

5. Compare *City of Boerne v. Flores,* 521 U.S. 507 (1997), and *Kimel v. Florida Board of Regents,* 528 U.S. 62 (2000), with *Katzenbach v. Morgan,* 384 U.S. 641 (1966).

Chapter 1. Accounts of Our Constitutional Practice

1. "In Suits at common law, where the value in controversy shall exceed twenty dollars, the right of trial by jury shall be preserved, and no fact tried by a jury shall be otherwise re-examined in any Court of the United States, than according to the rules of the common law." This relatively mechanistic provision guaranteeing the right to a jury trial is not so mechanical. There is a sophisticated and complex Seventh Amendment jurisprudence.

2. "All persons born . . . in the United States and subject to the jurisdiction thereof, are citizens of the United States and of the State wherein they reside."

3. 381 U.S. 479 (1965).

4. See Robert H. Bork, *The Tempting of America: The Political Seduction of*

the Law 257–59 (1990); Lawrence Sager, "Back to Bork," *New York Review of Books,* October 25, 1990.

Chapter 2. Judges as Agents of the Past

1. 15 U.S.C. 1.
2. 42 U.S.C. 000e-2(a)(1).
3. 42 U.S.C. 973(a).
4. See William N. Eskridge, *Dynamic Statutory Interpretation* 58–65 (1994). See also Cass Sunstein, "Interpreting Statutes in the Regulatory State," 103 *Harvard Law Review* 405 (1989). For an insightful discussion of the "speaker's meaning" theory, see Ronald Dworkin, *Law's Empire* 317–37 (1986).
5. "Justice Black and First Amendment 'Absolutes': A Public Interview," 37 *New York University Law Review* 549, 553–54 (1962).
6. See Scalia, *A Matter of Interpretation* 41–42 (1997).

Chapter 3. Enactment-Centered History as an Originalist Supplementation of the Text

1. Bork, *The Tempting of America* 144 (the emphasis is mine).
2. Michael Pollan charts the metamorphosis of *sweetness* and drolly notes that in the past "the word *sweetness* denoted a reality commensurate with human desire: it stood for fulfillment. Since then sweetness has lost much of its power and become slightly . . . well, saccharine." Michael Pollan, *The Botany of Desire: A Plant's-Eye View of the World* 17–18 (2001). An amusing mini-catalog of words whose meaning has drifted is provided in Bill Bryson, *The Mother Tongue—English and How It Got That Way* 77–79.
3. 347 U.S. 483 (1954).
4. See "Common-Law Courts in a Civil-Law System: The Role of United States Federal Courts in Interpreting the Constitution and Laws," in Scalia, *A Matter of Interpretation* 3; Ronald Dworkin, "Comment," in Scalia, *A Matter of Interpretation* 115, 120–22.
5. Consider the much-bruited example of the Fourteenth Amendment and the segregated schools of the District of Columbia: Professor McConnell has recently offered a revisionist history that emphasizes the deep opposition to segregated public schools felt by many of those most active in the shaping of the Fourteenth Amendment, and how close they came to outlawing segregation in the District of Columbia schools. Michael W. McConnell, "Originalism and the Desegregation Decisions," 81 *Virginia Law Review* 947 (1995).
6. See Christopher Eisgruber and Lawrence G. Sager, "The Vulnerability of Conscience: The Constitutional Basis for Protecting Religious Conduct," 61 *University of Chicago Law Review* 1245 (1994).
7. Once again the efforts of Professor McConnell—who comes to praise rather than bury originalism—offer good reason to doubt the originalist enterprise. In the most exhaustive historical dig to date, McConnell sets out the best

available evidence for the privileging view of religion, which he strongly favors. See Michael W. McConnell, "The Origins and Historical Understanding of Free Exercise of Religion," 103 *Harvard Law Review* 1409 (1990). But what that evidence amounts to is that the Titans may have disagreed: Thomas Jefferson had a relatively limited view, roughly comparable to what in modern terms would be an antidiscrimination stance towards religion; and James Madison had a more positive if somewhat ambiguous view, which on one possible reading would translate into a privileging approach towards religion. Once again, if we look for the understanding of the enacting generation as a whole, the screen of history is more or less blank.

8. My debt to Chris Eisgruber is great throughout this book. Here, in particular, I have been guided by conversations with him and by his excellent book, *Constitutional Self-Government* (2001).

9. This distinction owes an obvious debt to Ronald Dworkin. See Dworkin, "Comment," in Scalia, *A Matter of Interpretation* 115, 116–18; Ronald Dworkin, *Freedom's Law: The Moral Reading of the American Constitution* 13 (1996).

10. For a similar example, see Eisgruber, *Constitutional Self-Government,* 29–32.

11. 323 U.S. 214, 216 (1944).

Chapter 4. Three Rescue Attempts

1. Michael McConnell, "The Importance of Humility in Judicial Review: A Comment on Ronald Dworkin's 'Moral Reading' of the Constitution," 65 *Fordham Law Review* 1269, 1284 (1997).

2. Id. at 1286.

3. A representative statement of Lessig's approach can be found in Lawrence Lessig, "Fidelity in Translation," 71 *Texas Law Review* 1165 (1993).

4. A representative statement of Ackerman's approach can be found in Bruce Ackerman, *We The People: Transformations* 94–103 (1998).

Chapter 5. Enter Partnership

1. The March 2000 release of Albert P. Blaustein and Gisbert H. Flanz, eds., *Constitutions of the Countries of the World: A Series of Updated Texts, Constitutional Chronologies and Annotated Bibliographies* (1971–) contains entries for 192 countries. The United States is of course not the world's only constitutional role model; in particular, the influence of Kelsen and German constitutionalism should not be given too short shrift. See Bruce Ackerman, "The Rise of World Constitutionalism" 83 *Virginia Law Review* 771 (1997).

2. Eisgruber, *Constitutional Self-Government* 52–56.

3. See *Dolan v. City of Tigard,* 512 U.S. 374 (1994) (condition on building permit requiring landowner to dedicate portion of property for drainage and

public pathway constituted a taking; the findings upon which the city relied did not show a 'rough proportionality' between the condition and the proposed development); *Nollan v. California Coastal Commission*, 483 U.S. 825 (1987) (demand for public easement across lot in exchange for demolition and building permit was a taking, for there was no nexus between the legitimate state interest of maintaining ocean views and a condition of public access across a beachfront lot); *First English Evangelical Lutheran Church of Glendale v. County of Los Angeles*, 493 U.S. 1056 (1987) (landowner who claims that his property has been taken by a land-use regulation may recover for damages for the time before it is finally determined that the regulation constitutes a taking of the property); *Penn Central Transportation Company v. City of New York*, 438 U.S. 104 (1978) (refusal, pursuant to landmarks preservation law, to approve plans for construction of office terminal over Grand Central Terminal was not a taking of property, as it was not arbitrary or discriminatory, and did not interfere with the owner's present use or reasonable investment return).

4. This ignores the recent revival of interest in federalism and the separation of powers. This revival, however, is driven by interest in the allocation of power among governmental institutions and not justice per se.

5. Robert Nozick, of course, famously argued that no test of distributive justice grounded upon the resulting pattern of distribution was appropriate; rather, whether a distribution of resources was just depended wholly on the process by which people obtained these resources. Nozick, *Anarchy, State and Utopia* (1974). But Nozick's procedural view of distributive justice committed him to the principle of redress for past illegitimate appropriations, and our history is laced with reasons for doubt about the justness of extant distributions.

Chapter 6. The Thinness of Constitutional Law and the Underenforcement Thesis

1. Constitutional claims pointing directly towards minimum welfare rights have been systematically rebuffed. See, for example, *Kadrmas v. Dickinson Pub. Sch.*, 487 U.S. 450 (1988); *Dandridge v. Williams*, 397 U.S. 471 (1970).

2. 7 *Harvard Law Review* 129, 140 (1893) (quoting *Commonwealth v. Smith*, 4 Binn. 117 [Pa. 1811]).

3. Id. at 144.

Chapter 7. The Conceptual Salience of Underenforcement

1. 457 U.S. 202 (1982).

2. Id. at 221–23 (opinion of the Court); id. at 230 (Marshall, J., concurring); id. at 231–34 (Blackmun, J., concurring); id. at 238–39 (Powell, J., concurring).

3. 394 U.S. 618 (1969).

4. 415 U.S. 250 (1974).

5. This sense becomes stronger when *Shapiro* and *Maricopa County* are contrasted with *Sosna v. Iowa*, 419 U.S. 393 (1973) (upholding statute that required one year of state residency prior to petitioning for divorce), and *Starns v. Malkerson*, 401 U.S. 985 (1971) (upholding statute that required one year of state residency prior to eligibility for in-state tuition rates). The general sense that *Shapiro* signaled the Supreme Court's general sensitivity to the impact of durational residency requirements on the right to travel is made more credible by the voting rights cases which crowded behind *Shapiro*. See *Dunn v. Blumstein*, 405 U.S. 330 (1972). But the durational residency requirement and voting rights cases themselves are best understood as resting on the Court's distinct antipathy to the idea that would-be voters should marinate in local juices for a time before they are given the franchise. When the Court was satisfied that honest administrative concerns rather than local prejudice were at work, it rather casually approved the durational residency requirement in question. See *Marston v. Lewis*, 410 U.S. 679 (1973). For an astute effort to show the immanence of welfare rights in constitutional case law as of 1979, see Frank Michelman, "Welfare Rights in a Constitutional Democracy," 1979 *Washington University Law Quarterly* 659 (1979).

6. 526 U.S. 489 (1999).

7. 413 U.S. 528 (1973).

8. 413 U.S. 508 (1973).

9. 473 U.S. 432 (1985).

10. 531 U.S. 356 (2001).

11. Id. at 461 (Marshall, J., concurring in part, dissenting in part).

12. 397 U.S. 254 (1970).

13. 424 U.S. 319 (1976).

14. Id. at 340.

15. For an early lapse, see *Paul v. Davis*, 424 U.S. 693 (1976), where a flyer naming Davis as a shoplifter and sent to eight hundred local merchants was held not to implicate a liberty interest.

16. 419 U.S. 565, 584 (1975).

17. See, for example, *Whitney v. California*, 274 U.S. 357, 374 (1927).

18. 392 U.S. 409 (1968).

19. *Moose Lodge v. Irvis*, 407 U.S. 163 (1972).

20. *The Civil Rights Cases*, 109 U.S. 3 (1883).

21. Modest efforts to unearth the prompting of Justice Stewart's use of the word "relic" have not yielded fruit. But there are some venerable antecedents. John Stuart Mill, arguing that social stigma often outlasts the abatement of legal persecution, used the victimization of atheists as an example. Mill noted that the rule permitting only persons who believed in God and life after death to give evidence was one of the "rags" and "remnants" of the earlier persecution of nonbelievers. He lamented the rule as "a *badge* of hatred, a *relic* of persecution."

John Stuart Mill, *On Liberty* (E. Rapaport ed. 1978) p. 29 (emphasis added). W. E. B. DuBois described the "relentless color prejudice" that continued to handicap African-Americans in the wake of Abolition as a "relic of barbarism." *The Souls of Black Folk* (Signet Classic ed. 1995) p. 90.

22. 529 U.S. 598 (2000).

23. Id. at 625.

24. See generally, Richard J. Gellars and Murray A. Straus, *Intimate Violence* (1989).

25. 505 U.S. 833 (1992).

26. Id. at 888–92.

27. Gellars and Straus, *Intimate Violence* 31.

28. Id., citing Lenore Weitzman, *The Marriage Contract* 1–2 (1981); R. Emerson and Rebecca Dobash, *Violence Against Wives* (1979).

29. 521 U.S. 507 (1997).

30. 531 U.S. 356 (2001).

31. "Requires" in the present tense is apt here, because Title I of the ADA is still valid law, pursuant to Congress's authority to regulate interstate commerce. The importance of *Garrett*'s holding that Congress lacked Section 5 authority to enact Title I lies in the power of Congress when it acts under Section 5 to "abrogate" the immunity of the states against suits for monetary relief in federal court. After *Garrett*, all employers (including municipalities) except state governmental entities are vulnerable to suits in federal and state court for all applicable forms of relief under Title I. State governmental entities are vulnerable in state and federal court to suits for declaratory and injunctive relief under Title I, to suits for monetary relief in those state courts that do not hold their states to be immune, and even to suits for monetary relief brought by the attorney general of the United States.

32. *Garrett*, 531 U.S. at 382.

33. 426 U.S. 229 (1976). *Washington* famously held that a law's disproportionate burdening of racial minorities was not, in the absence of discriminatory motivation, grounds for application of the compelling state interest test.

34. 528 U.S. 62 (2000).

35. 416 U.S. 1 (1974).

36. 431 U.S. 494 (1977).

37. *Belle Terre*, 416 U.S. at 9.

38. 123 S.Ct. 1972 (2003).

39. The *Hibbs* Court itself distinguishes its sympathetic treatment of the FMLA from other post-*Boerne* cases on the ground that laws which discriminate on the basis of gender are subject to heightened judicial scrutiny, and, accordingly, that it is more plausible for Congress to find a pattern of unconstitutional state conduct when the welfare of women is at stake (and all the more so when it is the welfare of racial minorities that is at stake). But under prevailing doctrine, the mere disproportionate impact of a no-leave policy would

not justify heightened scrutiny and would not be unconstitutional. Thus, in *Massachusetts v. Feeney*, 442 U.S. 256 (1979), the Court measured a law granting veterans a preference in state employment against the permissive requirements of the rational basis test, and upheld the law, despite its grossly disproportionate impact on women.

Chapter 8. The Domain of Constitutional Justice

1. 334 U.S. 1 (1948). In *Shelley*, the Supreme Court held that the judicial enforcement of private, racially restrictive subdivision covenants constituted state action, and was thus subject to the Fourteenth Amendment.

2. I take this to be the starting point of Sunstein's sustained attack on "status quo neutrality." Cass Sunstein, *The Partial Constitution* 50 (1993). See also Cass Sunstein, "Lochner's Legacy," 87 *Columbia Law Review* 873 (1987).

3. 198 U.S. 45 (1905). *Lochner* struck down New York legislation specifying maximum hours for bakery workers, and is commonly identified as launching a period of three decades in which the Supreme Court acted to strike down economic regulations that it deemed inconsistent with free market outcomes.

4. John Hart Ely, *Democracy and Distrust* (1980).

5. 316 U.S. 479 (1965).

6. Dworkin, *Freedom's Law: The Moral Reading of the American Constitution* 15–26.

7. Frank Michelman, "Law's Republic," 97 *Yale Law Journal* 1493, 1535–36 (1988). In conversation, Professor Michelman has expressed some doubts about this aspect of his argument, which is why I am reluctant to assume his ongoing commitment to it.

8. A democratarian account of the Constitution need not equate the whole of the Constitution with the adjudicated Constitution; such an account could include judicial underenforcement of the Constitution. With the addition of this movable part, a democratarian account could be refined in several directions. Such an account, for example, might confine only judicial enforcement of the Constitution to the perfection of democracy and leave unadjudicated portions of the Constitution less fettered; or—more conventionally—it might maintain democratarian limits on the whole of the Constitution and distinguish between the judicially enforceable and judicially unenforceable portions of the Constitution on grounds of the likelihood that popular political institutions will arrive at constitutionally accepted outcomes. Admitting judicial underenforcement into the democratarian picture improves that picture, but the continued insistence on the hegemony of popular politics still causes difficulty. Confining either the reach of constitutional justice or constitutional adjudication to the perfection of democracy requires a justification that does not, I believe, exist—unless democracy is defined so broadly as to embrace the full concerns of constitutional justice.

9. Alternative formulations of the material dimension of constitutional justice surely merit attention. Prominent among the possibilities is a shift of focus away from minimum welfare per se and toward the opportunity to work and earn a decent wage. Sotirios Barber, for example, sees material well-being as a historically derived constitutional end that includes the individual's capacity to choose among vocations that promise income sufficient for decent housing, adequate nutrition, health care, education, and a secure old age. Sotirios A. Barber, "The Welfare State and the Nature of the U.S. Constitution: An Exchange of Views: Welfare and the Instrumental Constitution," 42 *American Journal of Jurisprudence* 159 (1997). Kenneth Karst has insisted on the material dimensions of constitutional justice in a number of illuminating essays; his most recent claim is for a judicially nonenforceable "right of access to work." Kenneth L. Karst, "The Coming Crisis of Work in Constitutional Perspective," 82 *Cornell Law Review* 523 (1997).

10. Correctly understood, our constitutional tradition of religious liberty centers on the project of protecting minority religious views from devaluation or discrimination, of ensuring equal liberty for all citizens whatever their religious commitments. See Eisgruber and Sager, "The Vulnerability of Conscience: The Constitutional Basis for Protecting Religious Conduct" 1245; Christopher L. Eisgruber and Lawrence G. Sager, "Unthinking Religious Freedom," 74 *Texas Law Review* 577, 600–614 (1996); and Christopher L. Eisgruber and Lawrence G. Sager, "Congressional Power and Religious Liberty after City of Boerne v. Flores," 1997 *Sup. Ct. Rev.* 79.

11. Infamy is almost always involved when a proper noun or a case becomes a verb.

12. Eisgruber and Sager, "The Vulnerability of Conscience: The Constitutional Basis for Protecting Religious Conduct" 1245, 1275–76.

13. See Dworkin, *Freedom's Law: The Moral Reading of the American Constitution* 15–26.

Chapter 9. The Birth Logic of a Democratic Constitution

1. There were, however, two interstate supermajority requirements: Article VII required the support of nine states (three-quarters rounded down) for the Constitution to take effect; and only those states which so ratified were bound (in effect a unanimity requirement).

2. While it is clear that the ratification of the Constitution was inconsistent with the terms of both the Articles of Confederation and the constitutions of the ratifying states, there is some debate as to whether the Constitution is best understood as having been illegal in its inception. Ahkil Amar argues that the Articles of Confederation created only external treaty obligations, obligations that were severed for all states when repudiated by any one state; as to the state constitutions, he regards these as having been understood as specifying nonex-

clusive means of amendment and implicitly embracing amendment by the popular sovereign of the relevant state by any appropriate means. Akhil Amar, "The Consent of the Governed: Constitutional Amendment Outside Article V," 94 *Columbia Law Review* 457, 464–70 (1994). Bruce Ackerman and Neal Katyal argue the Articles were a constitution for the United States and binding on all, and that most of those in the founding generation who concerned themselves with the question understood the launching of the Constitution to be illegal. Bruce Ackerman and Neal Katyal, "Our Unconventional Founding," 62 *University of Chicago Law Review* 465, 478–86 (1995). For my purposes, nothing turns on this nice question. Both Amar on the one hand and Ackerman and Katyal on the other take their respective readings of history to advance their respective versions of the claim that extra–Article V amendments to the Constitution are appropriate. I disagree, and my disagreement remains constant and, I think, equally strong as against either of these characterizations of the birth of the Constitution.

3. Familiar in rough, at least. Ahkil Amar, Bruce Ackerman, and Neal Katyal have done constitutional commentators a substantial service with their fine-grained reflections on the process of the Constitution's founding.

4. Bruce Ackerman used this phrase in conversation at a meeting of the Constitutional Theory Colloquium at New York University.

5. The most determined and elaborate attempt to find historical support for popular authority to amend the Constitution by non–Article V means is that of Bruce Ackerman. Ackerman points to the Founding, of course, and invokes the highly manipulated ratification of the Reconstruction Amendments and an unacknowledged New Deal Amendment as instances of the exercise of such authority. I have never failed to be engaged and educated by Ackerman's efforts to harness constitutional history in service of his project; but I have never been persuaded of its conceptual infrastructure, either. The Founding is a special case and can be justified on the far narrower grounds of constitutional breakdown, if justified at all. Reconstruction also courts understanding as a breakdown, of course, and is in any event garbled precedent for these purposes: After all, it was the importance of preserving the form of Article V amendment that drove the Reconstructionists to such questionable lengths. The New Deal conversion of the Supreme Court is the most interesting case, and here Ackerman's history is at best equivocal between there having been an informal amendment to the Constitution that obliged judges to follow suit, and what is commonly thought to have taken place, namely, a change in the prevailing judgment of the members of the Court as to the best understanding of the Constitution. In this choice between a positivist and judgmental account of the New Deal transformation, Ackerman could not possibly prevail without first persuading us of the normative claim underlying his interpretation—the claim that insists (in the closing words of one of his monumental efforts) that we must

strain to "leave a large space for the People, and their ongoing effort to take control of their government." At times, both Ackerman and Amar write as though they thought they could make their cases on grounds of "fit" alone, that the underlying normative claim is not essential. But interesting questions about the Constitution are seldom answered by text and history alone; and the claim for extra–Article V authority to amend the Constitution is in particular need of normative support.

6. Still more questions of the "voting-about-voting" sort are implicated in the election of delegates, of course.

Chapter 10. Democracy and the Justice-Seeking Constitution

1. At the turn of the millennium, the United Kingdom in fact finds itself acquiring a constitution by stealth. Transnationally, the United Kingdom, as a signatory of the European Convention on Human Rights, is open to the scrutiny and judgment of the European Court of Human Rights in Strasbourg. Nationally, the rights and freedoms guaranteed under the Convention are given significant weight in British domestic law by virtue of the Human Rights Act of 1998, which requires British courts to give legal effect to the Convention in legal disputes not implicating Acts of Parliament; to interpret Acts of Parliament so far as possible to make them compatible with the Convention; and—failing interpretive space to accomplish that—to declare those Acts to be incompatible with the Convention, thus triggering a fast track amendment procedure in Parliament. The Human Rights Act, though nominally merely a statute and with variegated force at that, is likely to come in time to function much as a judicially enforced bill of rights. Sub-nationally, authority recently has been devolved by statute from Westminster to parliaments or assemblies in Scotland, Wales, and Northern Ireland, thus creating a legally prefigured structure of quasi-federalism. Constitutional theorists, accordingly, will in future have only the memory of historic Britain as a counter-example to the flourishing of constitutionalism; parliamentary sovereignty is likely to become a theoretical possibility rather than a practical reality.

Australia is an example of judicially driven constitutionalism in a different form, which has resulted in what could be described as a *bill of rights by stealth*. Australia's written Constitution contains no express provisions analogous to the liberty-bearing provisions of the United States Constitution, but the High Court has recently held that some freedoms are implicit in the constitutionally mandated government structure. See *Australian Capital Television v. Commonwealth*, 177 CLR 106 (1992), deriving a principle of free political expression from the Constitution's commitment to democratic structures.

2. Jeremy Waldron, *Law and Disagreement* 16 (1999).

3. The apt phrases are from Frank Michelman, in the course of drawing

the distinction between "deliberative" and "strategic" politics. Frank Michelman, "Conceptions of Democracy in American Constitutional Argument: The Case of Pornography Regulation," 56 *Tennessee Law Review* 291–319 (1985). More generally, the broad model of popular politics that I am referencing here is often referred to as "deliberative democracy." In another, somewhat related context, Lewis Kornhauser and I have tried to draw and inform the distinction between preferences and judgments. Lewis Kornhauser and Lawrence Sager, "Unpacking the Court," 96 *Yale Law Journal* 82–117 (1986).

4. Bruce Ackerman, "Beyond *Carolene Products*," 98 *Harvard Law Review* 713–46 (1985).

5. My general debt to my former colleague Christopher Eisgruber is particularly strong here, as he has more than once pushed me to better understand and defend my view of this question.

6. Richard Fallon, "Foreword: Implementing the Constitution" 111 *Harvard Law Review* 56, 145 (1997). Professor Fallon expanded on the themes of this article in his valuable book, *Implementing the Constitution*, (2001). The compact treatment of the article makes it especially useful for my discussion, and I have accordingly confined my references to the article.

7. Id. at 148.

8. In *Washington v. Glucksberg*, 521 U.S. 707 (1997), Justice O'Connor lent her vote to Chief Justice Rehnquist's opinion describing the basis for denial of relief to those seeking the right to physician-assisted termination of their lives; her vote, in fact, was the fifth vote and hence necessary to make Rehnquist's opinion an opinion for the Court. But while Rehnquist's opinion defended a flat denial of any such right, O'Connor's concurring opinion was much more tentative in tone and pragmatic in its concerns.

9. When these words were first written, this possibility seemed distant, and therefore somewhat abstract. But, in the wake of the Supreme Court's decision in *Lawrence v. Texas*, 123 S.Ct. 2472 (2003), overruling *Bowers v. Hardwick*, and the subsequent decision of the Supreme Judicial Court of Massachusetts's decision in *Goodridge v. Department of Public Health*, 440 Mass. 309 (2003), declaring unconstitutional that state's bar to same-sex marriage, this discussion has a new cogency. The *Lawrence* case is discussed at some length in the Conclusion.

10. Fallon, "Foreword: Implementing the Constitution" 148.

11. Alexander M. Bickel, *The Least Dangerous Branch* (1962).

12. Gerald Gunther, "The Subtle Vices of the 'Passive Virtues'—A Comment on Principle and Expediency in Judicial Review," 64 *Columbia Law Review* 1, 3 (1964).

13. 410 U.S. 113 (1973).

14. 404 U.S. 71 (1971).

Conclusion

1. 123 S.Ct. 2472 (2003).
2. Tex. Penal Code Ann. §21.06(a) (2003).
3. 123 S.Ct. at 2484 (internal citations omitted).
4. 478 U.S. 186 (1986).
5. 123 S.Ct. at 2484.
6. 381 U.S. 479 (1965).
7. 163 U.S. 537 (1896), at 559.
8. *Goodridge v. Department of Public Health*, 440 Mass. 309 (2003), at 312.

Index